# PERFORMING FEMALE BLACKNESS

PERFO
FEMA
BLACK

# RMING
# LE
# NESS

Naila Keleta-Mae

**WLU PRESS** WILFRID LAURIER UNIVERSITY PRESS

This book has been published with the help of a grant from the Canadian
Federation for the Humanities and Social Sciences, through the Awards to Scholarly
Publications Program, using funds provided by the Social Sciences and Humanities
Research Council of Canada. Wilfrid Laurier University Press acknowledges
the support of the Canada Council for the Arts for our publishing program.
We acknowledge the financial support of the Government of Canada through
the Canada Book Fund for our publishing activities. Funding provided by the
Government of Ontario and the Ontario Arts Council. This work was supported
by the Research Support Fund.

Library and Archives Canada Cataloguing in Publication Data
Title: Performing female blackness / Naila Keleta-Mae.
Names: Keleta-Mae, Naila, author.
Description: Includes bibliographical references and index.
Identifiers: Canadiana (print) 20220452539 | Canadiana (ebook) 20220453012
     ISBN 9781771124805 (softcover) | ISBN 9781771124829 (PDF)
     ISBN 9781771124812 (EPUB)
Subjects: LCSH: Women, Black, in literature. | LCSH: Black people—Race identity.
     LCSH: Race in literature. | LCSH: Gender identity in literature.
Classification: LCC PN56.3.B55 K35 2023 | DDC 809/.933522—dc23

Cover and interior design by Lara Minja. Front cover image by Naila Keleta-Mae.

© 2023 Wilfrid Laurier University Press
Waterloo, Ontario, Canada
www.wlupress.wlu.ca

This book is printed on FSC® -certified paper, contains
post-consumer fiber and other controlled sources, is
manufactured using renewable energy - biogas and
processed chlorine free.

Printed in Canada

Wilfrid Laurier University Press is located on the Haldimand Tract, part of the traditional territories of the Haudenosaunee, Anishnaabe, and Neutral Peoples. This land is part of the Dish with One Spoon Treaty between the Haudenosaunee and Anishnaabe Peoples and symbolizes the agreement to share, to protect our resources, and not to engage in conflict. We are grateful to the Indigenous Peoples who continue to care for and remain interconnected with this land. Through the work we publish in partnership with our authors, we seek to honour our local and larger community relationships, and to engage with the diversity of collective knowledge integral to responsible scholarly and cultural exchange.

**Thank you** to my ancestors, family, and friends for the conversation, encouragement, and other generous acts of love that you have long offered me—it is an immense relief and tremendous honour to be in this world with you.

# CONTENTS

# ACKNOWLEDGEMENTS

Thank you to the Ontario Arts Council, Canada Council for the Arts, Social Sciences and Humanities Research Council, Ontario Ministry of Colleges and Universities, University of Waterloo, and York University for funding this research over the years.

Thank you to Senior Editor Siobhan McMenemy for her attentive and transparent stewardship of this process and thank you to the peer reviewers of this manuscript for their thoughtful and informative engagement with its academic and artistic components.

Thank you to my doctoral committee members Lisa Wolford Wylam, Leslie Sanders, Andrea A. Davis, Marlis Schweitzer, Gail Vanestone, and Ric Knowles for offering intellectual insights and space for creativity in the dissertation that evolved, in part, into this book.

Thank you to the faculty and graduate students I studied with at York University, the graduate students I taught at Goddard College, the undergraduate students I have taught at the University of Waterloo, and all the research assistants I have supervised—your questions and perspectives inform my own.

Thank you to all of the musicians, poets, theatre practitioners, film-makers, technicians, producers, and audiences I have collaborated with since I began making art in the eighties. Making art with you has shaped my understanding of the world and my place in it.

# 1

## FEMALE AND BLACK:
## A PERFORMANCE

**AS I WRITE THIS,** I am one and one-thirds full, thirteen weeks pregnant with the first fetus that I intend to carry to term. Laden with the enormity of this intention, I have avoided telling extended family and friends petrified by the possibility that biological unfoldings will trump the fulfillment of my intent. Simultaneously, the likelihood that my body will soon signal the heavily fetishized role of Black Mother disturbs me deeply. I vacillate between a deep and abiding desire to share the news and an equally visceral frustration that my expanding uterus will soon betray the controls I have learned to put in place over performances of my personal life in public.

Survival has become a heightened preoccupation of mine with each passing day. I suspect that my thoughts of survival are not musings on my present circumstances, but a heightened awareness of what is to come. In the days following their birth, my child's skin will deepen to a shade of brown that will identify them as Black when read along with the contours of their nose, lips, and hair in the geopolitical space that will most inform the early years of their life. As such they will be a member of the third-largest visible minority group on Turtle Island (on the lands also known as Canada) and the third-largest visible minority group in Tkaronto (also known as Toronto), the metropolis where they will likely be raised (Statistics Canada 2008, 5).[1] Will they be one of a few Black children in their daycare? Will their hair be a site of intrigue that children and adults comment upon and touch? Will they attempt to rub the brown from their skin? When will they ask me why we call ourselves Black when our skin is brown? When will my child shift from simply being in the world to attempting to see themself through others' eyes in the world? When will my inability to accurately recount our family's history beyond their great-grandparents fuse with their understanding of the broad scopes of imperial and colonial violence? When will they begin to understand that the Canadian national narrative includes limited articulation of the realities of people like their family members? When will they begin to feel and question the violent legacies and contemporary realities of misogyny and misandry in Black peoples' lives? Will they learn to perform to survive? How will I teach them to shift their performances into imaginative spaces of insight, power, and agency?

Over the years I have learned that inhabiting a body read as female and Black in contemporary Canada produces a relationship of suspicion with the world, one that constantly queries the premise of each interaction to parse the extent to which gender and race have defined its parameters and outcomes. I use the word "inhabit" as the description of my relationship with my body to mobilize a breadth of agency, while remaining cognizant of the Western and European Enlightenment-derived practice of representing female bodies as fragmented while promoting the existence of a whole, implicitly white, and male, self. However, my suggestion of the transformative capacity that inhabit signals is not meant to ignore the violence that is central to histories of female blackness in this country since the sixteenth century. Throughout this book, I also often place "female" before "Black" to foreground gender presentation as a primary site of inquiry and to interrupt the more common privileging of race over gender presentation that "Black female" or "Black woman" indicates.

The particularities of Canada's politics of gender, race, and nation are generally referred to as exemplary by disseminators of dominant discourse and divisive by those with limited access to dominant epistemological modes.[2] More specifically, as artists and scholars have expressed, female blackness as subject of inquiry is further occluded by the under-examination of the work of Black and other non-white scholars and artists in prominent Canadian scholarship and cultural production. As Djanet Sears points out in *Testifyin': Contemporary African Canadian Drama*, "there are serious patterns of omission in the documentation of African Canadian cultural production" (Sears 2000a, i). My research suggests that these patterns of exclusion occur because Black cultural production in Canada, as Alan Filewod observed within the context of Lorena Gale's play *Angélique*, "uses the moment of performance to destabilize the narratives that have historically secured Canadian nationhood" (Filewod 31).

At stake in the under-examination of Black cultural production in Canada is the opportunity to contemplate a geopolitical context where various ethnic, linguistic, national, and religious modes of blackness in general, and female blackness in particular, have collided for centuries. According to Statistics Canada's 2021 Census, 1.5 million people reported being Black. Within that Black population, 40.9 percent reported being born in Canada, 32.6 percent in Africa (including 7.1 percent in Nigeria, 2.8 percent in Ethiopia, and 2.4 percent in the Democratic Republic of the Congo), and 21.0 percent were born in the Caribbean and Bermuda (including 8.8 percent in Jamaica and 7.2 percent in Haiti) (2022, 21). Black people in these birth countries and regions generally share a common history played out on a common geographic terrain. This is not true for Black people in Canada, which is a decidedly heterogeneous population that "reported over 300 different ethnic or cultural origins in the [2021] census" (21). In this country, performances, and audiences of blackness in general, and female blackness in particular, vary widely for those of us who trace their lineage to, for example, Mogadishu, Somalia; Kingston, Jamaica; or Halifax, Nova Scotia. Those of us who inhabit bodies read as female and Black in Canada perform an array of understandings of female blackness while also performing for Black and non-Black audiences of various ethnicities. Yet Black, as an ethnic origin, facilitates a Canadian national imaginary that neatly flattens the details of an array of geographical origins of Black people into what is often referred to as the "Black community." In *The Dark Side of the Nation*, Himani Bannerji importantly instructs that the term "community" must always be contested: "[w]e need to remember that it is a political and cultural-ideological formation reliant upon social relations which are the base of social life, and not a spontaneous or natural association of people" (Bannerji 154). Inhabitants of bodies read as female and Black in Canada have long had to simultaneously value the specificities of our diverse cultural signifiers while fighting oppressive forces that seek to colonize our bodies and the spaces we occupy as human beings. Therefore, research and cultural creation about and by Black women and Black girls in Canada continue to be relevant scholarly and artistic endeavours within and beyond Canadian borders. This book seeks to contribute to these necessary academic and artistic conversations.

The central objective of *Performing Female Blackness* is to pursue the following lines of inquiry: What do contemplations of public and private performances of female blackness in Canada reveal about gender, race, and nation? And how does Canada, as a geopolitical site, shape performances of female blackness? My book asserts that those of us in Canada who inhabit bodies read by dominant culture as female and Black are always on stage. In other words, we constantly perform someone else's fantasies and/ or our own in the public and private spaces that constitute our everyday lives. Anti-Black racism, sexism, classism, and heteronormativity in Canada are the primary factors that necessitate this way of being and, as I theorize in this book, create the condition of *perpetual performance*. In short, I argue that people identified as female and Black are figuratively on stage regardless of the public or private stage space upon which we find ourselves. I argue that, in these conditions, performance becomes part of the ontology of female blackness in Canada.

I map this interplay of query, assertion, and theory through my own experiences of female blackness, which makes me not only the writer of this book, but also one of its primary subjects. My position as author and subject reflects my artistic practice, which predates my academic work. I follow the traditions of Black expressive culture established by Black female artists in Canada—such as Lillian Allen, d'bi.young anitafrika, trey anthony, Wendy "Motion" Braithwaite, Afua Cooper, and Althea Prince—and draw from personal and lived experience to shape and prioritize the artistic work that I make. This practice is not new. Black women in settings under heavy influence of Western modes of thought have long culled fiction, poetry, prose, narrative, and other writing forms from our experiences. I use the term "personal experiences" to signal my perceptions and memories of the various situations that have led to my present life, while I use the term "lived experiences" to signal stories that those in the communities I am connected to have shared with me.

In some instances, this book evokes the literary tradition of autobiography while, in other instances, it summons the relatively more recent anthropological intervention of autoethnography.

The positioning of myself as both writer and subject of this text is my effort to experiment at the crossroads of poetic and academic writing and blur the boundaries of autobiography and autoethnography. Both autobiography and autoethnography encourage a heightened level of critical self-reflexivity combined with the goal of telling larger stories while including one's own story (Duncan; Behar; Ellis; Keleta-Mae "*on love*"; Keleta-Mae "An Autoethnographic Reading"; McClaurin; Reed-Danahay). The ethical implications of this work can be challenging because an individual's personal experiences are inevitably deeply intertwined with other people's personal experiences. The questions that haunt those of us who write from personal and lived experience are familiar and numerous: Do I have the right to tell my story given that it intersects with someone else's life? If they are alive, should I ask for their permission to tell the parts of my story that implicate their stories too?

Strategies for how to navigate these, at times, tenuous spaces can be derived from examples of how widely known female Black artists and theorists have negotiated these terrains. For instance, not only did Audre Lorde draw constantly from personal and lived experience in ways that signaled autobiography, but she also introduced biomythography as a genre. bell hooks, though not positioned as a writer of autoethnography, often inserted family narratives and self-reflexivity into her research and writing. Zora Neale Hurston—an anthropologist who worked long before the term autoethnography was coined—integrated personal narrative into her work. In my experience, autobiography and autoethnography nurture self-reflexivity and a research methodology that provides dynamic insights namely into the questions that frame my research and how I value artists and theorists' observations about their work. My scholarly inquiry at times uses autoethnography as its methodology because it considers critical self-reflexivity as a viable and valuable theoretical and method-ological form of scholarship. And, while this book is not primarily an artistic endeavour, it is deeply influenced by my artistic practice that includes elements of self in its meaning-making and knowledge production processes.

The central contention of this book is that for those of us read as female and Black in Canada, intentionally identify moments, situations, and circumstances where we can shift our relationships with our bodies from *this is who I am* to *this is who I perform* reveals a deeply imaginative space. Throughout the book I identify *this is who I perform* and *this is who I am* as two possible locations on a vast spectrum of responses to the *perpetual performance* of female blackness that life in Canada demands. To be clear, my contention is that there are tensions and overlap between these two sites of theory and praxis, and I contrast them throughout the book to consider their limitations and possibilities. My claim here is that *this is who I perform* can be a subversive demonstration of agency—especially in non-Black and anti-Black spaces that demand performance as part of the ontology of blackness. In *Black Performance Theory*, D. Soyini Madison states that "With each generation, perhaps with each turn of a phrase, we stake a new claim within a new world order for the nature and significance of blackness" (vii). For me, *this is who I perform* stakes a "new claim" about how people who inhabit bodies read as female and Black in Canada can approach public and private moments in everyday life.

The performance of *this is who I perform* that I am theorizing is not prescribed; rather, the performance shifts depending on the audience, the performance space, and the epistemological contours of the context within which inhabitants of bodies read as female and Black in Canada wish to engage with their social and cultural statuses. Like many types of performances, these acts of intentional performance occur not only as physical articulations; they also become necessary for intellectual and cosmological survival in spaces dominated by European, Western, and Black nationalist epistemologies and ontologies. That said, *this is who I perform* and *this is who I am* are not meant to imply that a real, whole, stable self exists at the centre that is being denied or expressed in performance. Quite the contrary, *this is who I perform*, and *this is who I am* construct "I" from Trinh T. Minh-ha's perspective "[o]f all the layers that form the open (never finite) totality of 'I,' which is to be filtered out as superfluous, fake, corrupt, and which is to be called pure, true, real, genuine, original, authentic?" (Minh-ha 94).

I posit that conceptualizing the experience of inhabiting female blackness in Canada through the theory of *this is who I perform* facilitates the disruption of hegemonic notions of female blackness. In other words, my hope is that *this is who I perform* can function as an imaginative intervention that allows us to contemplate a world where Black women are able to freely live their own fantasies instead of performing those espoused by dominant cultures, both non-Black and Black. That said, I cautiously draw my construction of the liberatory possibilities of contemporary performances of female blackness in Canada cognizant of the history of performances that were forced upon Black people during and since chattel slavery. My assertion that *this is who I perform* has liberatory possibilities is not meant to ignore how performance and racial identification have been historically linked to force oppressive performances by inhabitants of Black bodies. Instead, I contend that *this is who I perform* can emerge as a personal politic that draws from the historical legacies of coerced performances while imagining new possibilities for performances of female blackness in daily life.

José Esteban Muñoz argues that "[t]he story of 'otherness' is one tainted by a mandate to 'perform' for the amusement of a dominant power bloc ... The minoritarian subject is always encouraged to perform, *especially* when human and civil rights disintegrate" (Muñoz 187). Muñoz also theorizes that some performances are acts of "disidentification" which is particularly productive when thinking about the potential impact of performances of female blackness on the "audience" and on the "performer" within and beyond the moment of performance. Muñoz writes, "[d]isidentification is about recycling and rethinking encoded meaning ... [it] is a step further than cracking open the code of the majority; it proceeds to use this code as raw material for representing a disempowered politics or positionality that has been rendered unthinkable by the dominant culture" (31). Within the Canadian context, "dominant culture" is not only shaped by the majority white mainstream but also by entrenched imaginaries of female blackness within Black communities. It is within these complementary and competing notions of female blackness that a shift from *this is who I am* to *this is who I perform* can emerge as an imaginative space rife with agency.

I assert *this is who I perform* as a preferred personal politic for inhabitants of bodies read as female and Black in Canada to conceptualize a relationship with our physical presence that is simultaneously cognizant of the historical memory our bodies conjure and imaginative about possible contemporary interpretations. My insistence on *this is who I perform*, particularly as opposed to *this is who I am*, is born of the material conditions of *perpetual performance* and has cosmological implications. In practical terms, how else to account for the acute difference of being a visible minority at Bayview Village Shopping Centre in Toronto, Canada, and an invisible majority at Rosebank Mall in Johannesburg, South Africa? In cosmological terms, how else to fashion words that touch and reveal expansive possibilities of female blackness that live just beyond violent images and discourses that plunge female blackness in Canada into an abyss of displaced humanity? And though it is beyond the scope of this research, it could be argued that performance as part of the ontology of female blackness could be applied more broadly in terms of what it considers (i.e., male blackness) as well as the geographical terrain it covers (i.e., North America). Thus, broader implications of this research include the examination of processes through which other minoritized bodies in Canada and beyond manage violent oppressive legacies and cleave open space through everyday performances to imagine Black life anew. And while Canada is this book's geographical terrain of inquiry, the research is also transnational insofar as it draws from artists and scholars from countries including Cuba, the United States of America, Jamaica, and Trinidad.

I turn to Black theorists beyond Canada throughout this book because national borders are porous constructions that did not contain chattel slavery or the diaspora that has consequently formed and, therefore, the blackness that emerged as a result also exceeds national borders. It is a blackness—a way of being known in the world and of knowing the world—that was constructed as ships carrying enslaved Africans traveled through waters that were also porous and borderless. In *In the Wake: On Blackness and Being*, Christina Sharpe carefully describes what would happen when a person who had experienced the horrific conditions of being enslaved on a slave ship was thrown overboard, as was routinely the case. Sharpe describes the types of motion they would experience as they moved through the wake of the ship, specifies that they would have quickly drowned and sunk because of little body fat to keep them buoyant, and writes of benthic organisms on sea floors that studies reveal pick whale carcasses clean in days (40). Sharpe asks, "What happened to the bodies?" and then responds, "because nutrients cycle through the ocean (the process of organisms eating organisms is the cycling of nutrients through the ocean), the atoms of those people who were thrown overboard are out there in the ocean even today" (40). I take solace in the assurance that the atoms of those who were thrown overboard and those who jumped move through bodies of water unbound by national borders. I now understand these waters as the graveyards of our dead circulating endlessly around the planet and through the atmosphere.

*Performing Female Blackness*, therefore, necessarily contemplates theoretical and artistic works by Black people beyond the nation-space of Canada because the atomic remains of Black life under chattel slavery are always circulating everywhere— lapping up on all nations' shores daily regardless of the extent to which they participated in chattel slavery or practice anti-Black racism today. This book also draws primarily from academic discourse emanating from performance, feminist, and critical race studies, and identifies my creative writing, personal experience, and lived experience as critical sites of theory. This unconventional form seeks to move through multiple registers of speech—from creative writing to academic prose—in its analysis of female blackness. Throughout the book, there are conventional academic sections that are intended to ground the research and its academic readers in familiar modes of scholarly communication. The other sections, however, seek to experiment with structure and style in unexpected ways that reflect my established practice of creating texts that integrate artistic and academic modes of intellectual engagement ("No Knowledge College," "An Autoethnographic Reading," "*on love*," "Writing with Sound"). My hope in bringing various forms of writing together in this book is two-fold: it will disrupt research, writing, and publication practices that are historically steeped in anti-blackness, and it will embody its title allowing it to read, in part, as an artistic performance.

In her poem "I'm Walking Out of Your Jail Tonight," dub poet Cherry Natural uses prison as a metaphor for colonialism. Natural imagines a protagonist who can permanently leave the prison when she wants to and does not need to flee because her freedom is not bound to court systems or restrained by prison guards. Instead, Natural creates a protagonist who announces her departure from prison in advance and makes clear her plan to simply walk away:

> I'm giving you back your Colonial attitudes,
> I'm giving you back your man-made rules.
> Take your laws out of my life,
> your standards are not mine.
> If it's the last thing I be I'm gonna be me.
> This spirit of mine must be free.
> So I'm walking out of your jail tonight.
> Yes, I'm walking out of your jail tonight. (44)

In this poem, Natural is walking towards freedom—a central pursuit of Black people since at least the advent of the transatlantic slave trade and during periods of colonization throughout Africa, the Caribbean, and North America. The difficulties of articulating freedom with language are brought into clear relief in the "Notanda" of M. NourbeSe Philip's *Zong!* where she says of language, "I distrust its order, which hides disorder; its logic hiding the illogic and its rationality, which is simultaneously irrational" (197). I feel a similar disease with English as expressed in my short unpublished poem "mother tongue":

am i meant to treat her
from whose womb i came
with the same disdain
that english has treated me?


enemy tongue.


english is my enemy tongue.

The conundrum for Black writers whose mother tongues are colonial is that we are using a language steeped in horror as the primary tool with which to imagine and articulate a world without the violence of anti-blackness. Like Philip, and Lorde before her, poetry and other forms of creative writing represent for me artistic ways to use colonial languages to disrupt colonial thought and practices. My intellectual engagement always includes art, not as an illustrative or tangential element, but as a vital and necessary form of meaning-making that enriches thought. To this end this book includes analysis of my poems "star" and "this is my rant" and my play *stuck* (2001) in Chapter 3; excerpts of my plays *No Knowledge College* (2007) and *What We Deserve* (2020); and sheet music for my song "Free"[3] (2020).

All my plays are dramatic explorations of Black theatrical traditions across the globe that emphasize the activist and transformative possibilities of theatre for practitioners and audiences. This is resonant in Canada, where Black communities have an established tradition of engaging in nuanced, sustained critiques of anti-blackness in dominant culture. For example, from 1840–43, Black people in Canada fought to impede the touring, across Canada, of minstrel shows from the United States that featured racist scripts and white actors in blackface (Breon 2). In her play, *The Adventures of a Black Girl in Search of God* (2000), Djanet Sears evokes this legacy of civic engagement through the characters of five Black senior citizens who go undercover as cleaning staff in order to ensure that Black artifacts in museums, country clubs, and private property are removed without detection, or, as they assert, are "liberated" (Sears 2000b, 530).

All my plays also focus on the dramatization of Black women's feelings, experiences, and fantasies. This emphasis reflects a rich tradition of foundational Black female theatre practitioners in Canada—including Lorena Gale, ahdri zhina mandiela, and Djanet Sears—whose early works established that inquiry into Black women's lives was a viable and valuable artistic contribution. Gale's play *Angélique* (1999) is a docudrama that restores and imagines the daily life of historical figure Marie-Joseph Angélique who was born into slavery in Portugal and sold into slavery in Old Montreal in the eighteenth century. mandiela's play *dark diaspora in dub* (1991), featuring seven women, was first performed at the Groundswell Festival by feminist company Nightwood Theatre and later presented at the International Women's Playwrights Conference (Lee). Sears won the Governor General's Literary Award for playwriting in 1998 for her play *Harlem Duet* about a Black woman who was the first wife of Shakespeare's Othello. My play, *No Knowledge College* (2007), is about a group of Black PhD students in Canada who accidentally discover that they are part of a federally funded study designed to develop, train, and produce graduates who will obtain high-level public and corporate roles but who will never disrupt the status quo. My other play, *What We Deserve* (2020), is similarly preoccupied with the conundrum of how to effectively and efficiently respond to anti-blackness and does so by revisiting characters from *No Knowledge College* many years later at a party to celebrate a distinguished speaker at a women's event earlier that evening. Instead they end up talking about an email sent from a disgruntled white female audience member.

I included my reggae song "Free" in this book because reggae music has a deeply rooted tradition of lyrics that express what centuries of violence have wrought on people—especially poor and working-class Black people. Ammoye Evans is a Jamaican-born reggae artist in Canada whose discography demonstrates rocksteady and dancehall reggae influences. Her song "Don't Count Me Out" from her album "The Light" (2017) tells a story of a girl born in tough economic and social circumstances who perseveres in the face of ongoing adversity. The critical analysis and relentless self-determination in her lyrics are enhanced by her smooth, soothing vocal delivery. Reggae music has always had a contingency of artists who provide sophisticated and scathing critiques of capitalism, colonialism, racism, and sexism in a range of lyrical styles (i.e., didactic, comedic, parabolic) and genres (i.e., rocksteady, dancehall). My dancehall reggae song "Free" follows these lyrical traditions:

Nuff corporations won't be outspent
Profit over people is too frequent
It's clear they don't want to live decent
These are facts we could not invent
Good life for all to the full extent
Not just the well-rich one percent
Condition nuh pretty cyaan content
So we rise up organize dissent

There's just one thing they must overstand
They can't expect people to be bland
Peace and justice go hand in hand
Freedom for all is our demand

Free from labels
Free from chains
Free is what we're born to be
And free we'll remain
(2020)

For at least the past century, inhabitants of female Black bodies
in North America have used creative writing as a transformative
expression of our experiences. Through poetry, those in bodies
read as female and Black have mobilized language to dismantle
dominant modes of thinking and envision the world anew. In
"Poetry Is Not a Luxury," Audre Lorde writes:

> I speak here of poetry as a revelatory distillation of
> experience, not the sterile word play that, too often, the white
> fathers distorted the word *poetry* to mean ... For women, then,
> poetry is not a luxury. It is a vital necessity of our existence.
> It forms the quality of the light within which we predicate our
> hopes and dreams toward survival and change, first made
> into language, then into idea, then into more tangible action.
> Poetry is the way we help give name to the nameless so it can
> be thought. The farthest horizons of our hopes and fears are
> cobbled by our poems, carved from the rock experiences of
> our daily lives. (37)

Consequently, scholars of female blackness in North America
have forged a rich tradition that treats the poetry of Black women
as informative sites of praxis and theory. The type of poetry I
feature in this book is performance poetry, which is a departure
from text-based poetry. My emphasis on performance poetry is
meant as an exploration of its dual emphasis on embodiment and
experience as expanded sites of meaning-making of female Black

subjectivity in Canada. I use the term "performance poetry" to encompass spoken word, dub poetry and rap poetry, three forms of embodied vocal performance that I have practiced in Canada, France, South Africa, and the United States since the mid-1990s. The genesis of my theory of *perpetual performance* is grounded in my creative writing, personal experience and lived experience as an inhabitant of a body read as female and Black in Canada and abroad when much of dominant discourse undermines female blackness as a nuanced site of humanity.

The work of scholars including Patricia Hill Collins, Carole Boyce Davies, Elaine Savory Fido, Hortense Spillers, and the Combahee River Collective indicates that experience is an integral epistemological component of female Black subjectivity. In *Black Feminist Thought: Knowledge, Consciousness, and the Politics of Empowerment*, Collins asserts that the:

> distinction between knowledge and wisdom, and the use of experience as the cutting edge dividing them, has been key to Black women's survival. In the context of race, gender, and class oppression, the distinction is essential. Knowledge without wisdom is adequate for the powerful, but wisdom is essential to the survival of the subordinate. (208)

In my experience, inhabiting a body read as female and Black in Canada creates a deep and abiding suspicion of large institutions that produce and claim authority over knowledge—such as public health, academia, art, law, and corporate media. Even a superficial transnational historical survey of such institutions reveals a racist misogyny that has, at various points, dissected female Black bodies, legislated them as reproductive objects, evaluated them as less than human, and portrayed them in systemically stereotypical ways. However, experience has taught me that it is reckless to solely value knowledge about female blackness that Canada's dominant institutions propagate as universal. In this country, children perceived as female and Black must learn to locate knowledge in academic crevices, wisdom from Black expressive cultures within and beyond Canadian borders and experiences from Black trans, Black female, and Black male people's lives. Collins' description of "experience as the cutting edge" dividing knowledge and wisdom exposes a space in which both can be contested and mobilized to articulate complexities and multiple subjectivities of female blackness (208). Within this space, creative writing, personal experience, and lived experience assemble themselves like a multimedia collage from which many inhabitants of bodies read as female and Black can fashion our lives. Therefore, I have chosen to simultaneously privilege creative writing, personal experience, and lived experience as sites of praxis and theory in this book to firmly position myself within traditions of Black feminist research methodologies. To that end, *Performing Female Blackness* incorporates my personal and lived experiences including some of my parents', Mae Belvett and Gerald Belvett, theories, and practices of blackness.

I use each of these ways of knowing (art, personal experience, and lived experience) to explore my argument that valuing and mobilizing multiple ways of knowing is a skill born of necessity once one realizes that they are read as female and Black in Canada. As is well documented, racialized feminists figure strongly in activist academic traditions, as does their clarion call for rigorous self-reflexivity. Within this self-reflexivity, scholars position themselves within their work through close examinations of how the various points of being that comprise their identity influence their research and interpretation. Western and European academic traditions, however, have generally sought to obscure the personal subjective impulses of their research and position their writing as that of the objective voice. My methodological choice to include creative writing, personal experience, and lived experience is meant to make the personal and subjective visible in my writing to align my research with those invested in the disruption of violent dominant discourse within the academy and beyond.

This book is particularly interested in how inhabitants of bodies read as female and Black approach and execute the translation of personal experience and lived experience into public performance. Glenda Dicker/sun, D. Soyini Madison, and Zora Neale Hurston are Black female scholars who understand and intentionally use their bodies as sites of public performances of a range of personal and lived experiences of female blackness for disparate audiences. Their acute awareness of their bodies is informative in understanding performance as part of the ontology of female blackness from audiences' perspectives. This information can then be used with awareness and performed with intentionality—as in *this is who I perform*. In "Festivities and Jubilations on the Graves of the Dead: Sanctifying Sullied Space," Glenda Dicker/sun describes her relationship with the source material she gathers through extensive interviews with community members to create a public performance: "I am the documentation. Within my body I hold the voices, sights, sounds, songs, that constitute the lives of these invisible people as they were told to me" (126). Dicker/sun identifies her body as the receptacle of community experience. Her source material is not solely in the notes she takes, the audio she records during interviews, nor is it in the objects she borrows for performance. Dicker/sun's body seems to absorb what is vital for performance and she is additionally able to prioritize others' stories through her body.

Similarly, in "Staging Fieldwork / Performing Human Rights," D. Soyini Madison succinctly describes the complexities of her positionality while seeking to create a performance from ethnographic research: "I am not the subject for subject's sake, but my subjectivity is a vehicle—it is of 'use value' to contextualize and historicize the Other" (402). Madison identifies her embodied female blackness as a conduit between the audience and those she has researched (the Other). She uses her body to create a context and history for "Other" people, which also seems to mean that Madison is interpretable by the audience as the Other (402). Madison's identification of her subjectivity as supportive to performance and not the primary driver can be productively contextualized by Mae Gwendolyn Henderson assertions in "Speaking in Tongues: Dialogics, Dialectics, and the Black Woman Writer's Literary Tradition." In it, Henderson provides a productive analysis of relationships between subjectivity and the Other in Black women's writing which she describes as an "internal dialogue with the plural aspects of self that constitute the matrix of Black female subjectivity" (18). In performances on stage, then, this "matrix of female Black subjectivity" can be understood to transform into an embodied "repository" (Dicker/sun 218) of personal and lived experience, and a medium (Madison) that connects the imagined Other and one's own otherness with the audience. The performances or displays of female blackness that emerge then are less about the actual person performing and more about the other subjectivities they foreground and prioritize in performance.

In "How It Feels To Be Colored Me" Zora Neale Hurston insists that "any act" of hers in her daily life in a body read as female and coloured—what most would now describe as Black—finds itself on a prominent "national stage" space with an audience that is unsure how to respond (153). Hurston writes, "[i]t is thrilling to think—to know that for any act of mine, I shall get twice as much praise or twice as much blame. It is quite exciting to hold the center of the national stage, with the spectators not knowing whether to laugh or to weep" (153). What is most pertinent here is Hurston's insistence that "any act" of hers occupies prominent "national stage" space and engenders audience response. What Hurston powerfully implies, then, is that her "stage" does not have to be an official, public space replete with costumes, lighting, paying audience and the like, nor do her "acts" require professional performance training or official performance contexts to be read as acts. Quite the opposite, Hurston asserts that she is always on a national stage and that all her acts are performances, including the mundane activities of her everyday life.

Hurston's acute awareness of gender, race, and nation is central to this research. Indeed, the controlled depiction of female Black bodies has been a preoccupation of nation states in North America and the Caribbean since the advent of the transatlantic slave trade. For inhabitants of female Black bodies, a contemporary heightened sense of a gendered and racialized body on the national stage emerges out of the brutality of this historical context. The material realities of this context are particularly difficult to negotiate in Canada where the dominant narrative of national identity vis à vis the transatlantic slave trade is that of Canada as the destination for travelers of the Underground Railroad. In "Nothing's Shocking: Black Canada," Katherine McKittrick calls the emphasis on Canada as the final destination the "safe-haven myth" and asserts that it is "one of the key ways in which the nation secures both its disconnection from blackness and its seeming exoneration from difficult histories" (119). Therefore, instead of having to discuss the existence of the chattel slavery in Canada, the dominant national narrative can focus on freedom. Given the insistent advancing of this "safe-haven myth" as the national narrative, the story of female blackness that emerges is one of exceptional strength as embodied by Harriet Tubman. It is important to underscore that Tubman, as the genesis of female blackness in Canada, locates the origins of blackness in Canada within the borders of the United States and consequently omits histories of Black people in Canada who were brought to labour as enslaved people or who migrated as labourers. What this incomplete rendering of the historical presence in Canada of female blackness specifically, and blackness more generally, achieves is the displacement not only of the existence of the slave trade in Canada but also of an accurate representation of historical Black presence.

The dominant national narrative that covers over Black presence has steadily been complicated and debunked most notably through artistic, historical, and academic analyses of the story of Marie-Joseph Angélique. Angélique was born into slavery in Portugal, accused of burning down the city of Old Montreal in Canada, and consequently tortured, hanged, and burned in 1734.[4] McKittrick argues that Angélique's existence destabilizes Canada's national narrative, "By exposing how transatlantic slavery played a key role in the making of the nation (through enforced labor and the entrenchment of racial hierarchies), Canada is exposed as both materially complicit to, and discursively innocent of, racial domination" (119). The advancement of the safe-haven myth through the body of Tubman, coupled with the covering over of the questionable torture and trial of Angélique, form the contours of the national stage of *perpetual performance* upon which inhabitants of female Black bodies in Canada are thrust. It is a national stage that requires people read as female and Black to perform freedom and deny violence to shore up the dominant national narrative. Questions that necessarily arise, then, are what happens to the Canadian fantasy of female blackness if the prominence of the narrative of Tubman and the Underground Railroad is replaced with the torture, hanging, and burning of Angélique? And how might notions of female blackness in Canada expand if both historical figures, Tubman and

Angélique, are equally mobilized and the historical presence of other Black people in Canada are brought to the fore?

In "The Economy of Violence: Black Bodies and the Unspeakable Terror," Bibi Bakare-Yusuf signals historical and contemporary material conditions that profoundly influence how Black people are viewed from within and without. Bakare-Yusuf asks, "What of the body that is always under the seduction of death, white racist violence, diseases, perverse heterosexism, pervasive addictions and unemployment? I am talking about the body that is marked by racial, sexual and class configurations" (313). My argument is that these markings culminate in the conditions of *perpetual performance* locating people read as female and Black always figuratively on the national stage regardless of the public or private spaces within which they find themselves.

European and Western philosophical, economic, cultural, and political movements have captured the imagination and transformed the material conditions of much of the world for the past few centuries. For example, Enlightenment, colonialism, and Modernity never asserted femaleness as exemplary of humanity. Quite the contrary, they debased femaleness and argued that females were without moral, cultural, economic, or political authority. Furthermore, each of these profoundly influential epochs of epistemological creativity made ontological claims that not only stripped blackness of authority, but also dehumanized it to advance the lie of whiteness, and white maleness, as synonymous with humanity. Within the vestiges of these palimpsestic legacies, as a Black girl in Canada I quickly learned that I was not the human "norm" and thus not privy to the historical, present, and future conceptual space that those who symbolize humanity, without qualification, enjoy. While a broad and nuanced array of responses to this arguably inevitable process of realization are available, creative writing, personal experience, and lived experience have taught me that they require some iteration of performance, one that locates female blackness within humanity.

This book asserts that this combination of historical and contemporary conditions is the *perpetual performance* that requires inhabitants of bodies read as female and Black in Canada to constantly perform other people's fantasies of female blackness in public and private spaces for spectators who are and are not white. It is important to note that the state of *perpetual performance* that I am theorizing is not prescribed; rather, the performance shifts depending on the audience, the performance space, and the epistemological contours of the context within which inhabitants of female Black bodies in Canada wish to manipulate status. Performance, then, is contemplated here for its ability to be mobilized as an act of political, economic, and social engagement. Like many types of performances, these acts of manipulation occur not only as physical articulations; they can also become necessary for intellectual and cosmological survival in spaces dominated by European, Western, and Black nationalist epistemological and ontological practices. More precisely, these internal and external material conditions occur in tandem and deeply influence what it means to inhabit and be viewed as female and Black in Canada in the mundane activities of private and public everyday life.

McKittrick argues that "black diaspora theories hold place and placelessness in tension, through imagination and materiality, and therefore re-spatialize Canada on what might be considered unfamiliar terms" (106). Similarly, my argument that structural oppression in Canada necessitates the *perpetual performance* of female blackness is not intended as a crude application of the word performance onto inhabitants of these bodies. Instead, *perpetual performance* is intended as an articulation that seeks to describe the persistent material conditions of public and private life along with the radical possibilities of performance. *Perpetual performance* offers performance as a way of understanding the endless daily pressures and demands on female Black life. In short, I am writing this book as a meditation on the imaginative possibilities that a shift from *this is who I am* to *this is who I perform* can reveal in living conditions that are shaped by a state of *perpetual performance*. My assertion is that people who are read as female and Black in Canada are always performing and that the ability to assess and respond to shifting circumstances and audiences creates space for multiple performance possibilities. I am attempting here to think and write about how agency has always been and is always present in the lives of those who inhabit bodies read as female and Black in Canada and the possibilities of a conceptual shift from *this is who I am* to *this is who I perform*.

In the second chapter, "Translucency," I posit the theory of translucency based on my analysis of my father, Gerald Belvett's, insistence that I "see a human being first" when I looked in a mirror at the Lacanian moment of misrecognition. In those moments I learned that humanity was not predicated on the gaze. It was not somatic. It could not be. Not for an inhabitant of a little Black girl's body living in Toronto, Canada, in the 1980s. If humanity was about the body, then there would have been little room for me to imagine much of anything beyond the tiny askew bits that dominant discourse and dominant culture portrayed of female blackness. I could feel the gendered and raced struggle that my mother, Mae Belvett, and others in bodies read as female and Black lived. My mother often says that she was not defined as "Black" until she came to Canada from Jamaica where hierarchical structures, though still steeped in European thought, were organized differently by the dominant culture. It was in Canada that my parents had to recalibrate their "oppositional gaze" (hooks 1992) as they experienced being seen and not seen or, as I theorize, being translucent.

In the third chapter, "Made Public," I examine how some performances can be augmented in professional performance spaces to allow for rehearsals of more expansive ideas about female blackness in everyday life. Through the analysis of two of my poems and one of my plays, the chapter considers the ways that femaleness and blackness impact the material conditions of each form and identifies some of the points at which they merge and diverge. Given its autobiographical and autoethnographic components, the chapter also emerges as an explicit engagement with the rich scholarly tradition of women, minoritized by Western constructs, who cull creative writing and critical interventions from personal and lived experiences.[5] *This is who I perform* requires constant reappraisals of differences between experience and perception. As a performance artist, watching videos and listening to audio recordings of my performances has enriched my practice, permitting me to identify discrepancies between my experience of my performance and my analysis of its effectiveness. The chapter "Made Public" makes public aspects of my process of revising my creative work.

In the fourth chapter, "Silence," I contemplate the historical legacy of the transatlantic slave trade on the lives of people who inhabit bodies read as female and Black through the analysis of Dionne Brand's acclaimed second novel, *At the Full and Change of the Moon*. I consider how the novel can be read as using silence as a literary device that not only accounts for the violence of chattel slavery and its far-ranging impact on the present, but also powerfully engages the reader's imagination. Brand's analysis is geographically expansive—she writes about enslaved people in the Caribbean and their descendants living in cities in Europe and North America. As evidenced by Brand's protagonist Marie

Ursule in Trinidad and her great-great-granddaughters, Maya in Amsterdam and Eula in Toronto, the legacy of the transatlantic slave trade "transfers" (Spillers 67) onto future generations even as they may attempt to distance themselves from it. In addition, "Silence" considers what is required to disrupt the hypervisibility of female blackness through examinations of the role of the body and the role of speech in everyday life.

In the final chapter, "A Letter," I reflect on how *perpetual performance* can demand performances of female blackness in everyday life that appear contradictory, including to the performer. In particular, the chapter draws from Patricia Hill Collins's inquiry into how Black motherhood can be experienced—from "oppressive," to "status in the Black community," to "a reason for social activism" (Collins 1987, 4). Through a brief analysis of the content and performance conditions of my poem "nine womyn," the chapter examines challenges that can emerge in communities of women who are influenced by and must grapple with systems of oppression at work within their organizing efforts. In addition, I reflect on my frustrations with my inability to consistently and successfully use *this is who I perform* to respond to misogyny and anti-blackness. This occurs, in part, because sometimes the moments are unexpected and brief, which is advantageous to those, unlike me, who are consistently able to respond quickly in the moment. The chapter concludes with a letter to my children.

## An excerpt from my play *No Knowledge College*

........................................................................

PORTIA       Maybe we can contact the media: newspapers,
             magazines, the CBC and CTV.

UMZANSTI     No credible media outfit will run this story
             without substantial proof and no one will
             corroborate the report but us.

PORTIA       Maybe we could occupy MOVE 86.9. Take over the
             university radio station and broadcast our story
             ourselves.

UMZANSTI     Then the focus would be on our rogue behaviour
             and not the substance of our complaint.

PORTIA       Maybe we should go international—contact the
             Human Rights Watch, they have an Academic
             Freedom Committee that deals specifically with
             academic censorship and ideological controls.
             We could also contact the Network on Education
             and Academic Rights. And there must be other
             relevant organizations, we just have to strategize,
             delegate and do some research tonight.

UMZANSTI     (*Looking at watch.*) When tonight exactly?

PORTIA       Now. We've got to do something. This is wrong.

UMZANSTI   Many things are wrong in the world Portia. The majority of the world suffers tremendously in excruciating circumstances, as the true minority indulges in whimsies. The study is unethical but it's not excruciating. We're not suffering.

PORTIA   My problem with your world view Umzansti, is that it always minimizes the potential for positive human impact on a specific situation.

UMZANSTI   Maybe once we're working we could gather information about the study from the inside, coordinate our efforts and assess the situation as an informed, rational collective.

PORTIA   Don't glamourize it Umzansti. We wouldn't be rational after a few months at cushy jobs we'd be complacent.

UMZANSTI   Don't talk to me about your revolution Portia. I've lived in the bloodshed, death, famine and astute poverty of "revolution" in South Africa. This is nothing, categorically insignificant in comparison to what the majority of the world faces daily. And you may want to consider the circumstances endured by the true world majority, it may help you contextualize your privileged Black Canadian meanderings.

PORTIA   Your who's-Blacker-than-whom intellectual arsenal is so worn out. Next you'll remind me for the billionth time, that your name means South Africa in Xhosa.

ZENZELE     We could sabotage the study.
            We could drop out of the program tomorrow.

77          But we're not like White people Zenzele, we can't
            teach in a university without a PhD no matter
            how much experience we have. We'll never be
            able to design any courses, never sit on a hiring
            committee, never become the dean of a faculty.
            We'll be radical and Black without credentials.

ZENZELE     We don't need PhDs to validate our existence.

SUNIFYA     I want my PhD and I want the $103,000 salary,
            four-week vacation and full benefits that CSIS
            is offering me. So, in three hours I will walk
            into conference room 406A[6] and defend my
            dissertation. Why? Because no matter what they've
            done, are doing or will do, I've earned my degree
            and every privilege that comes with it.

77          I think we need a safe place.
            Somewhere to raise children.
            Somewhere to think independent thoughts.
            Somewhere to self-actualize outside of someone
            else's agenda for us.

SUNIFYA     I think we need to be real. We at the plantation
            and we the house niggers collecting the scraps.
            We the updated, barely politically correct version
            of Tuskegee. That's just the reality. We're in the
            ivory towers, we know this system: it's a business:
            the commodity is social capital and they got what

I want. So please, don't fuck this up for me as you
navigate your middle-class Black nationalism.
Don't involve me, refer to me, don't include my
name in whatever you decide to do.

I need to get some sleep. Goodnight. (*She exits.*)

PORTIA   I'm writing a letter, tonight. I'm copying it to
every relevant media outfit, association and
organization that I can think of and tomorrow
I'm slipping it under every door and into every
mailbox I can find.

UMZANSTI   We're the subjects of a well planned and well
executed federally-funded study. You don't spend
a few hours in the middle of the night executing a
counterattack.

PORTIA   I'm sorry you feel that way Umzansti.
I see it differently.

UMZANSTI   What if you forfeit our degrees Portia? What if
they refuse to give them to us?

ZENZELE   I have to fight now Umzansti.
I don't know what else to do.

UMZANSTI   Wait!
Wait until we graduate.
Wait until we have our degrees in our hands.
Please.

PORTIA     They can revoke our degrees after they've been
           issued Umzansti. There is no guarantee.

(*Pause.*)

           I'm writing a letter and I'm distributing it as I see
           fit. That's what I have to do. (*She exits.*)

77         So what do we do?

CLAY       Find them and kill them.

(106–7)

# 2

# TRANSLUCENCY

**THIS CHAPTER THEORIZES TRANSLUCENCY** as a process by which those of us who inhabit bodies read as female and Black in Canada, are seen and not seen as we navigate the public and private social spaces of everyday life. This chapter explores the historical context and contemporary conditions that most inform why translucency emerges as an act of survival and disruption where *this is who I perform* replaces *this is who I am.*

In "Colonialism and the Birth of International Institutions," Antony Anghie traces the history of international law to argue that it was conceived and constantly revised to sustain colonialism. Anghie asserts that colonization projects entrenched in the development of international law anticipated and identified discourses that elicited the most resistance from colonial projects and colonial subjects. Once these sites of contestation were identified, international law was revised to subsume dissenting discourse through policy changes that permitted colonial practices to continue. For example, when competition among colonization projects led to increased militarism, international law was mobilized to rearticulate a shared agenda of economic gain through the narrative of "economic progress" because it was a "universal category" void of race or culture (Anghie 587). The inception of the Mandate System in 1919 is another example. Anghie argues that it "was not a departure from colonialism as

such; rather, it was a system of a progressive, enlightened colonialism, as opposed to the bad, exploitative colonialism of the
nineteenth century" (582). In these and other instances, the
relationship between colonization projects and colonial subjects
was mediated by policy changes in international law that used
the guise of an arms-length entity to cover over volatile aspects
of colonization without dismantling it.[1]

The effectiveness of international law relied on its being fused
with administrations, institutions, and other infrastructures that
secured the adherence of colonial subjects to the colonial regime.
This was important, for example, when liberalism forced violent
colonial practices to reproduce themselves as similarly brutal but
less visible policies of economic development. The policy focus
on economic development "led colonial powers to view natives
in terms of the labour and economic wealth they represented.
Simply put, the native was no longer merely to be conquered and
dispossessed; rather, he was made more productive" (Anghie 589).
In this instance, international law subsumed disruptive discourse
(in this case, liberalism, and humanism), renamed the colonial
subject "labourer" instead of "native," and rearticulated progress
as tied to moral individualism as opposed to amoral tribalism
(Anghie 590–91; 592n278). Within this insidious cycle, free individual labourers could track their economic progress by their
ability to participate in the free market, which, of course, still depended on the exploitation of their land and labour resources. To
this end, the native-cum-labourer-cum-free individual became
the central agent of their own exploitation through their collusion with the newly named but unchanged "system of economic
inequalities specific to colonialism" (Anghie 603).

Colonialism's epistemological assumptions are deeply embedded in Western culture. In her analysis of the term "postcoloni-
alism," Anne McClintock identifies ways in which postcolonial

study and postcolonial theory reproduce the same hegemonic discourse of linear progress through time that it seeks to rupture. According to McClintock, "colonialism returns at the moment of its disappearance" (11). It is precisely because of colonialism's ability to disappear and return in the same instant that a female, Black, heterosexual, working-class person becomes at once possible and necessary in Canada. Indeed, she can only exist in this seemingly nuanced way—gendered, racialized, sexualized, and classed—because of colonialism's capacity to subsume disruption and reproduce its epistemes through its imbrication with administrations, institutions, and other infrastructures that nurture the collusion of colonial subjects with colonial regimes. Indeed, my articulation of the cultural signifiers that most constitute how female blackness is read in Canada is a production of the same system of colonial epistemes that at various historical moments conflated female with reproductive property, Black with primitive,[2] sexual with hypersexual, and middle-classed with field nigger. If, in each of these historical moments, human beings in bodies like mine believed that we were what dominant culture described us as, we would have only recently become human beings worthy of the same human rights as the most powerful among us.

Personal and lived experience has taught us that it would be foolish to fully embrace the language used to describe Black people in these times because that, too, will likely change, as evidenced by linguistic incongruities throughout Canadian history that have at different times identified Black people as niggers, Negros, Black Canadians, African Canadians, Afro-Canadians, and the like. If in each historical instance human beings in physiognomies read as Black believed dominant nomenclature, we would be at the behest of the whims of dominant discourses that we have not controlled. My assertion of *this is who I perform* emerges in response to these conditions, while being cognizant of the historical relationship between Black people and what were often coercive performances to satiate imperial fantasies. Certainly, the colonial era is fraught with stories of Black people being forced to participate in an array of humiliating performances to survive.[3] Arguably, the most prominent story is that of Sarah Baartman, the so-called "Venus Hottentot" born in 1789 in what is now South Africa, and who was exhibited on stages, cages, and private parties in London and Paris by 1810. Deborah Willis's *Black Venus 2010: They Called Her "Hottentot,"* analyzes the implications of European fascination with Baartman, in life and death, for contemporary times.

*This is who I perform* identifies that which already exists—the imagination that those in bodies read by society as female and Black have used to endure in moments when dominant culture has treated us as less than human. *This is who I perform* is my conjecture, a leap of imagination, to envisage, for example, how Baartman may have been able to subvert her reality and perform an image without *being* the image,[4] to be seen and not seen, to perform what I call translucency. The theory of translucency makes apparent that performance is part of the ontology of female blackness in anti-Black, patriarchal contexts. Therefore, when those who identify as female and Black approach these contexts cognizant of translucency, *this is who I perform* can be used as a response through which sexism and anti-Black racism can be interrupted, subverted, and resisted. In this regard, *this is who I perform* can emerge not only in homage to the possibility that the creation of conceptual space demanded from inhabitants of female Black bodies throughout colonialism but also as means to practice imagination as a transformative expression of possibility. Furthermore, *this is who I perform* is deeply tied to Black feminist efforts to create epistemologies that articulate worldviews that are grounded in our personal and lived experience.[5]

In "On Being the Object of Property," Patricia J. Williams depicts the experiential processes through which neocolonial subjects theorize being looked at by gazes that (re)produce them as objects:

> My parents were always telling me to look up at the world;
> to look straight at people, particularly white people; not to
> let them stare me down; to hold my ground; to insist on the
> right to my presence no matter what. They told me that in this
> culture you have to look people in the eye because that's how
> you tell them you're their equal ... What was hardest was not
> just that white people saw me ... but that they looked through
> me, that they treated me as though I were transparent. (160)

In Williams's theorization of transparency, the neocolonial subject's gaze confronts that of the neocolonizer and within this collision, the system of colonialism is regenerated such that the image reflected to Williams is not a body but an object—specifically, "a thin sheet of glass" (161). bell hooks also theorizes her personal experiences of being instructed by her parents about how to look at adults. In "The Oppositional Gaze: Black Female Spectators," hooks describes being reprimanded as a child by her parents for staring at adults with an unwavering intensity that was perceived as a challenge to authority. The punishments she received for staring in this way taught hooks that to gaze was a political act, one that embodied the "power in looking" (115). hooks then connects the historical practice of white owners during chattel slavery punishing enslaved Black people for staring with her experience of being punished by her Black parents as a Black child. Referencing Michel Foucault, hooks identifies the repetition of punishment in Black parenting as a reproduction of a strategy of domination that in fact created in Black people a greater, more resolute desire to look. hooks calls the looking that results from attempts to repress

Black people's right to look an "oppositional gaze." She writes, "By courageously looking, we defiantly declared: 'Not only will I stare. I want my look to change reality.' Even in the worse circumstances of domination, the ability to manipulate one's gaze in the face of structures of domination that would contain it, opens the possibility of agency" (116). As a child, my father would often stand beside me in front of the bathroom mirror and tell me that when I looked in the mirror, I needed to see more than my skin colour. He would say that I needed to "see a human being first." My parents lived in Jamaica while it was legally a British colony, and as such they were intimately familiar with the material conditions of being a British colonial subject. When they moved to Canada in the 1960s, the U.S. Black Power, civil rights, and feminist movements were growing, and my parents experienced how they were largely ignored by dominant Canadian discourse effectively maintaining the hegemonic colonial legacies that developed the Canadian state.

Citing the colonial contexts of Ruandi-Urundi and Belgium and the East India Trading Company and British Empire, Anghie describes a "commonplace colonial strategy" wherein colonies paid for infrastructure projects that extracted resources for the Empire's gain (599–600). By the time I was born my parents understood—through material conditions in Canada—that Canadian colonization projects misconstrued blackness to produce neocolonial subjects necessary for their own exploitation. My father's insistence that we work in the mirror together was a disruption of the reproductive capacities of colonialism—his pedagogy led to my theorization of translucency. I learned through our work in the mirror that my humanity existed not in tandem with my skin colour, but somewhere *before* any expression of my body. The core disruptions then were epistemological, ontological, and teleological; "see a human being *first*," he would say. I have no memory of my father mentioning my gender in these moments in the mirror; thus, he implicitly identified gender as a site of invisibility that either could not be changed or needed not be changed. Instead, he focused on skin colour and emphasized the perspective attained when a person was able to gaze at her body and, more specifically, at the materiality of her own face. I call my father's theory of seeing oneself as a human being first "translucency." In a performance of translucency staged in front of a mirror, the neocolonial subject gazes into the mirror, sees a reflection, and inserts the filter of human being into the reflection *before* they acknowledge it as their own. For a neocolonial subject read as female and Black, the performance of translucency has broader implications. It can impact her experience of looking at others and of being looked at by Black and non-Black people in ways that can interrupt the transparent neocolonial gazing that Williams describes (160).

In "Beyond Miranda's Meanings: Un/silencing the 'Demonic Ground' of Caliban's 'Woman'," Sylvia Wynter illuminates the political and conceptual implications of the shift from sexual difference to racial or physiognomic difference that Western Europe enacted and manipulated to sustain its "dazzling rise to global hegemony" (Wynter 358). Specifically, Wynter identifies the existence of a necessarily imaginative space that is demarcated by non-white women through the writing and critiquing of Caribbean literature. Wynter describes this intellectual space as "demonic ground" and contends that it offers a new way of conceiving of humanity. Referencing the essays in the collection *Out of the Kumbla: Caribbean Women and Literature*, Wynter constructs her chapter as an example of this space and depicts it as:

> [P]rojected "demonic ground" outside of our present
> governing system of meaning, or theory/ontology in [A.T.]
> de Nicolas' sense of the word that it is precisely the variable

"race" which imposes upon these essays the contradictory
dualism by which the writers both work within the "regime
of truth" of the discourse of feminism, at the same time as
they make use of this still essentially Western discourse to
point towards the epochal threshold of a new post-modern
and post-Western mode of cognitive inquiry; one which
goes beyond the limits of our present "human sciences,"
to constitute itself as a new science of human "forms of
life." (356)

Wynter explicitly locates "demonic ground" outside of
dominant feminist epistemes, and furthermore identifies it
as a space attainable by those whose feminist inquiries overtly
work with the complexities of race. According to Wynter, it is
the consideration and analysis of race that forces those invested
in this work not only to grapple with implicitly white Western
feminist discourse, but also to envision "new post-modern and
post-Western" epistemes. Certainly, embedded within Black
feminisms' English-language discourse in North America and
the Caribbean is an acute consciousness of terrains of white
Western discourse. My contention is that a deep awareness of
tenets of white Western discourse is not only a mode of survival
for many scholars but is also necessary for those invested in the
praxis of improving Black life. Indeed, the work of many scholars of female blackness in North America and the Caribbean is
deeply engaged with efforts to reconstruct fields of inquiry. These
scholars pay careful attention to the pervasive legacies of white
Western discourses' violent history of attempting to collapse and
contain female blackness. It is noteworthy that Wynter chose
the term "demonic ground" as a counterpoint to Luce Irigaray's
use of "silenced" ground (qtd in Wynter 355). Wynter's choice of
"demonic" evokes the Christian idea of Satan and the demons

who serve him. Given the prevalence of Black feminisms in the aforementioned geopolitical spaces, Wynter's evocation of demons reminds me that feminist scholarship is also engaged in the analysis of Christianity and other religions.

I was raised in the United Church of Canada. I was raised by Christians to be a Christian; I went to Sunday School, sang in choirs, and played piano during offertories and processionals. The services were short, and the musical ministry focused on traditional renderings of hymns. Though my parents were raised in predominantly Black churches in Jamaica, the congregation they chose in Canada was predominantly made up of middle-class descendants of white Europeans and middle-class-aspiring, non-white, first-generation Canadians raising young children. Some Sundays I went to my maternal grandmother, Beryl West's, Pentecostal church, where the vast majority of the congregation was comprised of Black people, mostly from the Caribbean. They talked often about Satan and how he was always conspiring to lead people astray and that only faith in God could hold Satan at bay. My grandmother's church services went on for hours, singing was lively, and parishioners shook tambourines, testified, and sang lively renditions of songs like "The Center of My Joy" by Richard Smallwood.

The two prominent stained-glass windows at the church where I was raised feature images of a tall, slim Jesus with wavy shoulder-length dirty blond hair, a narrow straight nose, light-coloured eyes, and cream-coloured skin. In one stained glass window Jesus is alone. In the other, there are children around Jesus and the children have features and skin colours that signal Asian, Black, and European ethnicities. My father sat on the committee that chose the stained-glass windows and was instrumental in the inclusion of non-white children. He argued that the church could not attract or retain people of various ethnicities if we were not included in its institutional imagery. The inclusion of children of various skin colours in those two stained glass windows was a big deal for our growing church in a developing suburb in Toronto in the 1980s. In our community, it felt like a sign of liberalism and progress because it visually institutionalized the Canadian national narrative of multiculturalism that was heightened at the time. It must be underscored that even with the liberal, progressive imaginary that the stained-glass windows represented, the most prominent and powerful in the image was that of a white, male Jesus.

I remember that the cover of the big white hardcover Bible in our living room at home had a large swath of torn paper and glue residue where an image had been. My parents explained that there had once been an image of a white Jesus that they had torn off before sharing the bible with their children. I never actually saw it but knowing what had been there and what they decided needed to be removed resonated more powerfully than actual seeing might have—Jesus's visual absence loomed large. I was never confirmed as a teenager, never reaffirmed the baptismal vows my parents took on my behalf when I was baby—I just could not wrap my head or heart around having a white male Jesus and a male God at the center of my faith.

In "Stylin' Outta the Black Pulpit," Grace Sims Holt asserts that the Black church in the United States emerged out of white immorality that sought to satisfy two arguably competing goals with the shared aim of securing white people's quick entry into heaven. Firstly, to frame the status of human being as something enslaved Black people could only achieve in heaven and secondly to position the giving of Christianity to enslaved Black people as a symbol of the white people's devotion to God. According to Holt, the principal function of the Black church from the per-spective of white owners of enslaved Black people was the pursuit of economic gain—specifically, because Christianity was meant to contain and pacify enslaved Black people and thus ensure productivity, reduce resistance, and increase profits. Holt argues that the Black church that developed responded primarily to enslaved Black people's psychological needs for an affirmation of earthly self-worth and dignity, an explanation for incomprehensible Black suffering, a promise of punishment for white persecutors, and the pursuit of economic power. In addition, Holt highlights a telling irony that illuminates the historical context within which Christianity emerged as a powerful cosmological counter-discourse through which Black people who were enslaved found revenge, retribution, and justice. Holt writes,

> What a white witness could never conceive is that the man who can never enter the kingdom of God is the *white* man. The flock understands this with crystal clarity ... The propertyless slave or Black (take your pick) was incapable of being guilty of the sins of greed, avarice, gluttony, callousness, brutality, and hypocrisy ... A white heaven was virtually abolished by definition since, also by definition, very few whites could meet the admission standards. (336)

The following hymn, "Got a Home in That Rock," aptly describes Holt's assertion:

> I've got a home ina that Rock,
> Don't you see?
> I've got a home ina that Rock,
> Don't you see?
>
> Between the earth and sky
> Thought I heard my Saviour cry,

I've got a home ina that rock,
Don't you see?
Poor old Lazarus, poor as I,
Don't you see?
Poor old Lazarus, poor as I,
Don't you see?

Poor old Lazarus, poor as I,
When he died had a home on high,
He had a home ina that Rock,
Don't you see?

Rich man, Dives, lived so well,
Don't you see?
Rich man, Dives, lived so well,
Don't you see?

Rich man, Dives, lived so well,
When he died he found a home in hell,
He had no home in that Rock,
Don't you see? (Lindsley 49)[6]

Regardless of whether one has been formally raised in a Black church in the United States, its tropes and symbols resonate as a communicative mode of blackness, especially for those in North America and the Caribbean who trace their lineage through the transatlantic slave trade. For example, in "Sounds of Blackness Down Under: The Café of the Gate of Salvation" E. Patrick Johnson discusses how Black American gospel music was appropriated and performed by a majority white, secular Australian gospel choir. Johnson focuses on the aspects of Black American gospel music and culture that the Australian choir used as entry points to shared meaning. In the Canadian context, Breon argues that the Black church played a central role in the development of Black theatre practitioners because the church functioned not only as a religious institution but also notably as a social one: "It would be difficult to number the many actors, singers, musicians and dancers who had their first taste of performance by way of the local church" (Breon 1). Consequently, because the church created a regular stage-space for artistic expression, it is also reasonable to assert that the Black church was deeply influential in the development of Black audiences and Black performance aesthetics in Canada. As such, as head of the church, Black preachers were well-positioned to have a wide and largely undocumented impact on the development of Black artists, aesthetics, and audiences while also experimenting with and refining their own performance practices where autobiographical narratives of self can be woven into performances from the pulpit. Further, accomplished preachers pay close attention to their audiences, assess their needs, and determine the extent to which it is in the preacher's interest to meet or resist those needs. Within dominant Black imaginaries of Black churches in North America, the accomplished preacher offers a compelling example of authoritative public performance. The lesson—for those who inhabit bodies read as female and Black who seek to use *this is who I perform*—is that we can deploy some of the aesthetics and practices of Black preachers and churches because of their resonance and legibility with Black audiences.

I remember the women at my grandmother's church. They often caught the spirit, fell to the floor, wept, and were covered and lifted by the attentive arms of their church sisters. I was at once terrified and enthralled by their witnessing and testimonies. I wanted to try. I too wanted permissible space to wail, moan, and be incoherent, comforted and touched by the Holy Spirit and quietly attended to by church women. It was the only context I had ever seen where inhabitants of female Black bodies in Canada were socially allowed, by themselves and others, to transgress the borders of the femaleness and blackness that (from my vantage point as a child) governed much of their lives. These days I accept that I am not a Christian, despite the significant and meaningful theoretical work that feminist theologians have done. Too much of Christianity's theology must be suspended or rendered invisible for me to worship faithfully in the physical form that I inhabit in contemporary Canada. I use "inhabit" because I have experienced the confusion and the anger that performing translucency have afforded me, and these days my questions require the conceptual imaginative space that the word "inhabit" suggests. Simultaneously, "inhabit" is also meant to signal the work of understanding the dynamics of this lived reality. Indeed, my use of "inhabit" to describe my relationship with my body gestures towards a separation or distinction from the physical and signals a cosmological relationship—one that seeks to occupy the "demonic ground" that Sylvia Wynter argues is outside of hegemonic discourse.

Though Wynter does not specify white in her use of the term Western in her article "Beyond Miranda's Meaning: Un/silencing the 'Demonic Ground' of Caliban's 'Woman,'" I would argue that white is implied. I have chosen to make white visible in the following passages of writing to overtly disrupt the invisibility that is often a key characteristic of whiteness. Not only is white Western meant to signal white people, but it is also meant to gesture towards the many Westerners and Europeans who are not white and who may or may not traffic in white Western and white European thought. I am attempting to tease out the nuances of modes of meaning-making that are racially identified to signal their ideological genealogies and thus the power structures most at play. In this case, those of us who mobilize white Western epistemes and ontologies would not necessarily racially identify as white. As such, I am using white Western to signal all of us who uphold power structures created by white Western ideologies that assert and sustain dominance.

English-language theorists of female blackness in North America and the Caribbean suggest numerous perspectives from which to manipulate white Western discourse and disrupt rationalism's systems of understanding. Of note are intersections in works by Barbara Christian, Patricia Hill Collins, the Combahee River Collective, Kimberlé Williams Crenshaw, Andrea A. Davis, Angela Davis, Audre Lorde, Hortense Spillers, and Sylvia Wynter. When specific works by these scholars are read together, two frameworks of analysis emerge that are especially productive for this research: language as an identifier of non-demonic ground, and new ontologies of Black feminism. In conversation with Wynter's description, I use "non-demonic ground" to signal white Western discourse, especially liberal and progressive feminist scholarship, that gazes at female blackness in ways that ignore our agency and rights to our bodies (Davis 2005, 107). To be clear, it is not only attentiveness to race that makes feminist discourse part of Wynter's "demonic ground" as I interpret it. Instead, it is the meaningful engagement with race, agency, rights (Davis 2005, 107), wisdom, knowledge, and experience (Collins 1990, 208) that make it possible to theorize from the "demonic ground" which lies "outside of our present governing system of meaning" (Wynter 356). Embedded within the texts of many of the theorists is a counter-discourse, an oppositional force that the texts explicitly and implicitly name. It is this force that represents the "non-demonic."

An overt example of the identification of limitations of white Western feminist discourse is posited by Crenshaw in

"Demarginalizing the Intersection of Race and Sex: A Black Feminist Critique of Antidiscrimination Doctrine, Feminist Theory, and Antiracist Politics." Crenshaw states:

> The value of feminist theory to Black women is diminished because it evolves from a white racial context that is seldom acknowledged. Not only are women of color in fact overlooked, but their exclusion is reinforced when *white* women speak for and as *women.* The authoritative universal voice—usually white male subjectivity masquerading as a non-racial, non-gendered objectivity—is merely transferred to those who, but for gender, share many of the same cultural, economic and social characteristics ... Consequently, feminist theory remains *white,* and its potential to broaden and deepen its analysis by addressing non-privileged women remains unrealized. (46)

Here, Crenshaw clearly identifies the ethnic and gendered terrain of white Western feminism (non-demonic ground), the violence imbedded in the limitations of its analysis (the authoritative universal voice), and the locations where the "demonic ground" exists (potential of analysis of non-privileged women's lives).[7] The Combahee River Collective offers an implicit example of how to identify the non-demonic in their article, "A Black Feminist Statement." The Collective states, "We believe in collective process and a nonhierarchical distribution of power within our own group and in our vision of a revolutionary society. We are committed to a continual examination of our politics as they develop through criticism and self-criticism as an essential aspect of our practice" (218). Through its articulation of its beliefs, the Collective uses tactically different language than Crenshaw to locate itself within the "demonic ground" and imply about white

Western discourse much of what Crenshaw lays bare. Presuming its implication of white Western binary thought, the Collective's emphasis on "a nonhierarchical distribution of power" infers the existence of an individual, hierarchical, capitalist, and imperialist white Western status quo. Lastly, the Collective contrasts white Western society's chronic under-examination of historical and current political practices with the Collective's forwarding of their commitment to "self-criticism." For example, by virtue of its name and its decision not to include a list of the names of its individual members in the publication, the Combahee River Collective also identifies a group voice as a central component of inhabiting "demonic ground" and subsequently integral to any imagining of what Wynter describes as "a new science of human 'forms of life'" (356).

In "The Race for Theory," Barbara Christian complicates both the explicit and implicit linguistic approaches that Crenshaw and the Collective respectively employ through her analysis of manipulations of language for political gain. Writing within the context of a then-emerging movement in critical theory in the United States in 1988, Christian observes:

> I feel that the new emphasis on literary critical theory is as hegemonic as the world it attacks. I see the language it creates as one that mystifies rather than clarifies our condition, making it possible for a few people who know that particular language to control the critical scene. That language surfaced, interestingly enough, just when the literature of peoples of color, black women, Latin Americans, and Africans began to move to "the center." (71)

Christian importantly identifies the existence of an elite academic minority with power expansive enough to shift the direction of an entire field of scholarly inquiry. Furthermore, through her use of quotation marks, Christian throws into question the meaning of "the center" and destabilizes the circular framework of analysis prevalent in white Western discourse whereby the centre is most powerful and the periphery of little influence. Though Christian implies the sex, race, and class of the "few" elites she chides of hegemony, like Crenshaw, Christian is explicit in her identification of which aspects of white Western discourse she seeks to interrogate. While in the preceding quote Christian is not overtly invested in articulating the terrain of the "demonic ground," she is productively thoughtful in her capacity to signal a larger systemic cycle of how linguistic inroads into the "demonic ground" are captured by a few and subsumed to regenerate empire. Within this insidious cycle, as access to the "demonic ground" is gained by those interested in non-white people's lives, "a few" remap the non-demonic through their creation of a new language that charts the playing field anew and disrupts borders that once marked where the demonic began.

There are numerous popular culture examples of the vicious cycle of existing language being manipulated to forward an oppositional voice to dominant discourse which is then co-opted or rendered obsolete by dominant discourse in ways that drastically undermine, if not mock, the impetus of the initial effort. Terms including "cultural diversity" and "political correctness" stand out as prime late-twentieth century examples in a North American context. The former has come to signify an anti-white masculinist left-leaning agenda, while the latter has become a code word for a harmful form of self-censorship. At the very least, one must ask: How did activist efforts for cultural inclusion and expansion of centres of power become taboo? How did calls for self-reflexivity with attention to political contexts come to exemplify a betrayal of self-expression? Whose interests are best served when language is repurposed in these ways? It is helpful here to recall Anghie's illustrations of how international law (and the colonial administrations, institutions, and infrastructures it serves) was used to anticipate and subsume dissent through policy changes. Furthermore, as Anne McClintock succinctly and disturbingly asserts through her analysis of the term postcolonial, "Colonialism returns at the moment of its disappearance" (McClintock 11).

When inhabitants of bodies read as female and Black perform translucency in daily life, we can manipulate moments of return and disappearance. We can perform audiences' expectations of us being transparent while simultaneously remarking borders in subtle ways that blur elements of *this is who I am* in ways that extend our playing fields of possibilities. Like an established Black preacher who knows their audience well, performers of female blackness can adjust their performances to pose questions that will haunt patrons in quiet post-performance moments when the primacy of performers' rehearsals of the familiar fades. Billie Holiday provides a productive example of how this can be achieved. In "'Strange Fruit': Music and Social Consciousness," Angela Davis analyzes the material conditions in which Holiday popularized "Strange Fruit"—the haunting poem of lynching in the United States of America. Davis analyzes the impact of Holiday's decision to perform "Strange Fruit" between love songs in the middle of her set helped challenge the notion of a divide "between fame and commercial success on the one hand and social consciousness in music on the other" (Davis 184). Davis observes that, "[i]n the popular imagination, lynching was the established order's ideological affirmation and corporeal destruction of Black hypersexuality. Because of the historical linkage of sexuality and freedom in Black culture, Holiday's decision to foreground 'Strange Fruit' in her musical oeuvre accorded her love songs a richly textured historical meaning" (Davis 195). To this end, while the content of Holiday's set remained the same, its structure shifted the meaning of the entire performance. This is an informative lesson for people read as female and Black who use *this is who I perform* to manage anti-blackness, sexism, and the like. Holiday's experiences identify the importance of autonomy in framing performances of female blackness. It is not always about creating new material (i.e., new songs for Holiday to perform); sometimes it is about reframing material that already exists.

Wynter observes that a pressing issue is that of "the ontological difference and our *human* and *'native' human* subordination, hitherto non-conscious, to the governing behaviour-regulatory codes of symbolic 'life' and 'death'" (365). Through her use of quotation marks in the term "*'native' human,*" Wynter signals the perpetual outside position that white Western discourse and its practitioners impose on those whose ontologies fail to reproduce white maleness or white femaleness. Wynter asserts that *human* and *"native" human* are both inferior locations when it comes to female blackness because both are sites of subordination in systems of meaning governed by maleness and whiteness. She suggests that regardless of evolutions in language usage that signal equality (i.e., female Black people are human, too), the word "human" has also continued to evolve to hold a hierarchical range of meanings that consistently devalue female blackness. This conundrum is not easily solved, as Christian illustrates in her description of the few at the centre who attempt to obfuscate fringe movements through the creation of new theories and newly encoded language. Within this complex environment of *perpetual performance*, translucency emerges as a mode of survival, transgression, and transformation. Within these power struggles, performances of translucency assert and manipulate "human" as a viable location even as some posit that the only available human status for female blackness is one that is subordinate to all other human beings. Wynter argues that what emerges from this tenuous space is a "new metaphysical imperative" that requires a "second self-assertion," one that is intriguingly disinterested in attempts to modify what she describes as an individual's "nature," but focuses instead on changing entire modes of meaning-making (365). In other words, it is not the "nature" of the performer of female blackness that needs to change, but the ways in which her performances are understood by herself and by her audiences. Understanding her relationship with her body as *this is who I perform* instead of, for example, *this is who I am,* opens space for Wynter's "new metaphysical imperative" (Wynter 365) because it is, indeed, a new "self-assertion"—one that interprets the borders of physiognomy anew.

Nonetheless, the impacts of the legacies of colonialism and chattel slavery on Black life are personal and political. The violent erasure of humanity that chattel slavery and colonialism demanded can result in a debilitating and discombobulating mêlée of shame, insecurity, and anxiety for people read as female and Black in North America.[8] Williams writes,

> There are moments in my life when I feel a part of me is missing. There are days when I feel so invisible that I can't remember what day of the week it is, when I feel so manipulated that I can't remember my own name, when I feel so lost and angry that I can't speak a civil word to the people who love me best. Those are the times when I catch sight of my reflection in store windows and am surprised to see a whole person looking back. Those are the times when my skin becomes gummy as clay and my nose slides around on my face and my eyes drip down to my chin. I have to close my eyes at such times and remember myself, draw an

internal picture that is smooth and whole; when all else fails,
I reach for a mirror and stare myself down until the features
reassemble themselves like lost sheep. (165–66)

Like Williams, I have spent time in the mirror attempting to
assemble myself. The time I have spent there has been in search
of an image that was recognizably human in the moments when
the legacies of colonization and chattel slavery have derailed
my father's insistence that I insert "human" into my gaze.
Simultaneously, however, it is in these most tenuous moments
that translucency has generated new epistemes to contest the
destruction empires require. They are epistemes that have sought
to radically disrupt the reflected gaze of the neocolonial subject
back to themselves and the gaze of the neocolonial subject
towards the neocolonizing subject in ways that have the potential
to produce new perceptions of what constitutes human beings.

Translucency's preoccupations with how concepts of what constitutes human bodies are generated and consolidated is of import
when considered in relation to Williams's argument regarding the
complex relationships between images, rights, and power,

> In the law, rights are islands of empowerment ... Rights
> contain images of power, and manipulating those images,
> either visually or linguistically, is central in the making and
> maintenance of rights. In principle, therefore, the more
> dizzyingly diverse the images that are propagated, the more
> empowered we will be as a society. (170)

Drawing from Williams's theorization, translucency's focus on
the manipulation of visual images of human is a complex assertion of rights wherein the body can perform an image of itself as
powerful. The performance of translucency is a process through

which the un-righted use colonial systems of rights to violently write/right images of power before/over their bodies.[9] It is a performance in which neocolonial subjects implicitly accept the violent colonial episteme that the image immediately reflected back is not human. In other words, when an inhabitant of one of the bodies in question looks in the mirror, there is a moment of misrecognition,[10] an instant when they see their reflection and do not see a human being. Translucency attempts to distort the power of the image through a transcendence of the physical that separates "human" from all perceivable bodies.

As discussed earlier in this chapter, colonialism continually necessitates moments where colonial subjects embody narratives and fantasies of their separation from the violence of colonialism. To suggest that one is complicit or to understand one's body as that of a colonizer is to project a violent construct onto one's inner sense of self, locating one's body in brutal histories with contemporary implications. To see bodies as sites of translucency where our bodies *are* our borders *and* are porous is to see imaginative space in moments that colonialism attempts to foreclose. *This is who I perform* seeks imaginative space to perform translucency *without* appropriating or becoming empire. *This is who I perform* uses the premise of translucency to satiate colonial projects' desires for visible, governable bodies, without requiring the performing bodies to desire themselves "outside" of themselves to become someone else. To perform translucency is to perform at the border in the sense that Ursual Biemann asserts in "Performing the Border: On Gender, Transnational Bodies, and Technology:"

> Tracing new paths that blur with the first winds, she crosses the border, moving in and out of legality. Hers is not a one-time kind of crossing with the aim of becoming someone else on the other side. Rather, she is a subject in transit,

> moving through the transnational zone while finding ever-new
> strategies to get around the prevailing power structures on
> her clandestine trajectory. (112)

Translucency then is not a suspension of the corporeal, it is the flexibility of performing colonization's legacy of female Black transparency and knowability based on assessments of the histories of brutality in nuanced material spaces. Translucency is also then not a suspension of humanity—it is a disruption of colonialism while remaining cognizant that the ammunition required to fight is not equitably distributed. Instead, translucency perceives space in the inner and imagines the inner as material for performance. It is an ontology of female blackness that imagines the physical form as able, through performance, to radically create performances of one's body as self. In "Diaspora, Citizenship and Gender: Challenging the Myth of the Nation in African Canadian Women's Literature," Andrea A. Davis articulates the perils of an unresolved, untraceable lineage for ontologies of female blackness. Though Davis is not directly engaged with Wynter's work in this article, Davis nonetheless sounds a telling and cautionary note in her description of an equal rigidity within spaces that Black feminisms might create and conceive of as "outside our present governing systems of knowledge" (Wynter 356). Davis writes, "The realities of disconnectedness, fragmentation, and homelessness encoded within the diaspora experience often also encourage people of African descent to rely on their own constructions of black identities guarded within equally rigid notions of identity, nation, and belonging" (Davis 2004, 65). In this regard, Davis highlights the complexities of Wynter's "demonic ground" through her description of its epistemic ties to the white Western and white European discursive *inside* that it seeks to disrupt. Likewise, performances of female blackness as static inside and outside of spaces are threatened in everyday life. They are subject to the same perilous possibilities of stagnation, repeating white Western and white European discursive regimes and/or embodying dominant notions of blackness.

Christian's prior-mentioned observance of cyclical patterns of linguistic manipulations emerges here as a useful framework of analysis. As Black diasporas redefine blackness, multiple modes of expression of blackness emerge and, inevitably, movements at the centre attempt to determine the direction of blackness. This is also often accompanied by their attempt to erect and police borders of blackness, borders created in response to Black people's perceptions of non-Black people's projections of us. This cycle is well documented in the Black Arts Movement in the United States of America that sought, for example, to police blackness that was not heterosexual, patriarchal, male, and nationalist.[11] This was also the case in South Africa's Black feminist movements, which were collapsed into dominant liberation discourse as oppositional to and separate from the larger, allegedly more important, nationalist movement.[12] In "Fear of a Black Planet: Rap Music and Black Cultural Politics in the 1990s," Tricia Rose contemplates meanings of Black people in performance within the context of rap music. Rose differentiates between visible and invisible aspects of Black performance and identifies their commonality in the political implications of performance. Rose writes, "Rap's poetic voice is deeply political in content and spirit, but its hidden struggle—that of access to public space and community resources and the interpretation of Black expression—constitutes rap's hidden politics" (Rose 289). In Rose's account, possible meanings of Black performance and Black culture in general are determined within the interplay of visible performance ("content and spirit") and its invisible material conditions ("access" and "interpretation").

Rose frames the relationship between rap's visibility and invisibility within a larger conversation about attempts in dominant culture to police and contain Black people and Black life. Interestingly, Rose identifies a lack of access to attentive artistic criticism as integral to the analysis of the material conditions that limit possibilities of Black performance. She argues that meanings of Black people in performance are fractured into at least two camps based on the audience's capacity to identify the "deeply political" aspects of the performance's "content and spirit." Rose asserts that the relationship between Black performers and their audience is integral to any analysis of a performance's possibilities and limitations. Like Holt's assertion that the Black preacher used shared racialized experiences to create meaning with their Black congregation, Rose argues that when performers and spectators are Black, registers of meaning become available that a heterogeneous racial context would foreclose.

Michael Eric Dyson offers a perspective that is also helpful in understanding the relationship between Black performers and their audiences. Dyson asserts that "there are instances of both black complicity and black resistance in the commodification of the black cultural imagination, and the ideological criticism of exploitative cultural practices must always be linked to the language of possibility and agency in rendering a complex picture of the black cultural situation" (Dyson 413). Dyson's observation is a sage reminder that conversations about meanings of performances by people read as female and Black must be located firmly within the larger context of advanced capitalism that dominates North American and Caribbean life. It is by no means a new phenomenon for Black people and Black life to be commoditized; however, the present brand of commodification provides insights into the changing dynamics between Black performers, Black audiences, and larger societies. Certainly, people read as female and

Black are implicated in the complex shifts in meaning, performance, and possibilities that the market dictates and that we influence based on our investments in femaleness and blackness. In
particular, people read as female and Black are constantly challenged to negotiate these investments as we analyze the impact
and reception of our performances on the series of nuances that
form our mundane everyday lives in a hyper-capitalist state.

In "The Fact of Blackness" (a compelling example of performative writing published long before performance studies coined
the term), Frantz Fanon invites readers to contemplate the profound grief that emerges as a confluence of his embodied experiences of blackness. Fanon writes, "Yesterday, awakening to the
world, I saw the sky turn upon itself utterly and wholly. I wanted
to rise, but the disemboweled silence fell back upon me, its wings
paralyzed. Without responsibility, straddling Nothingness and
Infinity, I began to weep" (Fanon 1967, 140). In Fanon's narrative, tensions between material possibilities and limitations are
palpable, particularly because he posits that it is a result of logic
without reason ("disemboweled silence"). What Fanon intriguingly asserts is that his tears stem from the realization that he
is "without responsibility" and thus without historical or future
context. Theorists of female blackness specifically and blackness
more generally at times take up the notion of responsibility within the context of the state of Black families, Black communities,
and Black masculinity. However, what Fanon suggests is that responsibility is a compulsory component of humanity, and that
the manifestation of humanity is decidedly not an option for
those "fixed" presumably in or by blackness.

Informed by Fanon, Dyson, Rose, and Biemann's analyses,
I theorize translucency as an understanding of one's body as a
scrim or a filter that unfixes itself from *this is who I am* through
performance. For inhabitants of bodies read as female and Black,

translucency is about being looked at by spectators with shared gendered, racialized experience and being looked at by spectators without that experience—both of which generate gazes that can make female blackness feel like a "thin sheet of glass" (Williams 161) or like it can be "dissected" (Fanon 1967, 116). But translucency is also about the inhabitant of a body read as female and Black looking with a gaze that, hooks asserts, "opens up the possibility of agency" (hooks 1992, 116). Furthermore, translucency is about paying close attention to audience composition and seeks shared experience (like the Black church and rap music) to increase possibilities for meaning-making. Translucency takes seriously the ability of colonialism to reproduce itself through colonial subjects, institutions, administrations, and infrastructures (Anghie) and its capacity to return and disappear in the same instance (McClintock 11). Therefore, my theory of translucency seeks to disrupt colonialism through the assertion of *this is who I perform*.

I have entered a place of deep reflection over the past months. The reality of feeling life becoming more and more of itself inside of me is making life feel too precious for the pretense of compartmentalization that adulthood seems to demand. These days I feel entrenched in life's messiness, buoyed by its magnificence, and simultaneously devastated by its constant tragedy. I am twenty-nine weeks pregnant now and I am falling in love with being pregnant, with the ways in which it is moving me to be present and in my body. I am falling in love with feeling parts of my baby's body nudge against the sides of my uterus. I have become enamoured with the feel of my mother's hands rubbing my belly and the tone of her voice as she greets her grandchild. I love when my husband places his face near our baby in my uterus and tells them, "We love you." I was not expecting this. I had not anticipated that I would be so curious about who the person growing inside of me is, nor had I considered how much I would feel the need to support them as they do whatever they are coming to the world to do. On the dedication page of her book *The Salt Eaters*, Toni Cade Bambara writes about her mother, "who in 1948, having come upon me daydreaming in the middle of the kitchen floor, mopped around me." Most days I find myself hoping that I will have the presence of mind and humility of character to give the person inside of me space. I hope to create a safe place for them where they can learn a breadth of performance skills that they can translate into currencies of communication that will expand the possibilities of their life.

# 3

## MADE PUBLIC

**THIS CHAPTER'S RESEARCH METHODOLOGY** uses my published text "star," my recorded performance poem "this is my rant," and my produced play *stuck* as departure points to discuss official performances of female blackness. The pieces I have selected for analysis were, at the time of their creation, challenging for me to share publicly because each required a performance of female blackness that I felt transgressed acceptable borders of sex and race. Furthermore, each piece uses first-person singular often, regardless of biographical accuracy. On official stage spaces, audiences generally perceive "I" as autobiographical—an assertion of *this is who I am*—unless the performer indicates a sex, race, or age that is difficult to read as their own. It becomes more complex to assert *this is who I perform* in a context where a performer uses "I" and audiences, understandably, think it is an accurate portrayal of the person performing. This chapter explores some of the informative tensions between *this is who I am,* and *this is who I perform* in these instances.

I wrote "star" in 2002 after returning from my first trip to South Africa and in response to an email from Ntone Edjabe about what he called the "New South Africa." Our exchange was subsequently entitled "Bantu Serenade" and published in the magazine *Chimurenga*. "star" was written in a then-nascent performance poetry practice in Canada that evolved into the more widely known genre of spoken word while remaining referential to its early influences of performance art, rap, and dub poetry. Many Black artists in Canada were drawn to the possibilities of this experimental performance practice. This is evident in the publications *T-Dot Griots: An Anthology of Toronto's Black Storytellers*[1] featuring close to forty poets and *The Great Black North: Contemporary African Canadian Poetry*[2] that features more than ninety poets. This is poetry that generally critically engages with prominent issues in Black communities and explores a range of aspects of Black life. It is also work that is often focused on advancing the liberation of Black people—an impetus that at times takes on pedagogical qualities as evidenced in the collection *Live from the Afrikan Resistance!* by El Jones, a prominent Black spoken word artist in the country. The first of four sections in Jones's book is entitled "The Ancestors" and it is comprised of sixteen poems, most of which are introduced by a paragraph or two that shares a little known fact about the subject matter, a personal anecdote about the subject matter's relevance to the author, and/or historical information about the person named in the title (i.e., "Toussaint L'Ouverture" and "Viola Desmond"). This careful and thoughtful framing provides the reader with additional information and subsequently with more ways into understanding each poem's content and subject matter and through this gesture, Jones foregrounds poetry as instruction—a pedagogical tool that can advance Black liberation. My poem, "star," shares similar concerns about liberation through its examination of material excesses and ethical quandaries of middle- and upper-class Black people in North America and Southern Africa. Written from the perspective of a Black woman in Canada in her twenties, this long-form poem delves into the interplays of class, sensuality, sexuality, and gender in movements for Black liberation.

## star

........................................................................................

shit.

now what the fuck am i supposed to do with that?

why ya got to go and kill the dream? i'm not trying to hear
that folks are jumping through similar hoops a continent away.
damn. that's supposed to be the motherland. that sweet sweet
place called home. that place where i and millions of other lost
children of the african diaspora can go to just "chill out" not have
our brains spill out on pavement/cement tenements the same way
it is here.

(i need a space where i can grow out of harms way/i'm black
u see.)

just last night i was reasoning limeing with a bredrin/writer/
poet friend, discussing how toxic north america is and how
imperative it is that we bounce as often as possible to maintain/
attain some semblance of perspective (yes, nothing like financial
privilege). continually bombarded by propaganda machines.
numb. the natural result of excessive north american condition-
ing. numb, i am. close to being immune too. politics slip so easily.
chant down babylon one minute, surf the net to price my future
luxury vehicle the next, complete with tan leather interior and
brown tinted windows (not Black—that's far too ghetto.) fuck.

struggling i am. enticed by the perceived beauty and the allure
of that sweet Black suburban bourgeoisie. and what's the alternative? actually live the politics i spew in "conscious" social circles?
damn all that "revolution of self" talk makes me nauseous. i'm
trying to be like bob—well at least like buju, so i can talk about
the struggles of poverty when i'm straight rolling. why can't i
just be profiling? u know, make nuff loot and have nuff access to
comfort before i get too stressed out about global details.

conveniently conscious sister. looking for a conveniently conscious significant other so we can sit back, relax and listen to the 8-track. let's talk about the sign o' the times. maybe unwind over a bottle of good south african red wine, make love until the sun sets again and revolutionize the world sprawled out on plush couches after a delicious three course meal. I'm saying. I'll wear my army fatigues to keep it real, some old school darkers, phat boots and a fine leather jacket by day. (night-time's private.)

lawd a mercy

wha gwan? ah dat mi wan fi know.

i feel so fucking inadequate. and somewhere inside i know there isn't enough stuff in the world to make me feel better, but i'll probably die before i stop trying to buy my way out of emptiness. how much do i have to unlearn and how much work do i really have to put in? ah hell. sick just thinking about it. lonely. i am. lonely. fly body, fairly steady mentally and no one to invest all that love energy into. it sucks, you hear me. i don't even know if i have the energy to talk politics, discuss world issues, drop names, show how well read i am, be "deep" as i negotiate my way into a whole other club of the conscious conscious really conscious black crew. you know, the one that's super critical of most mcees for not keeping it real enough. you know, the crew of readers/thinkers that chant down babylon with proper colonial english sophistication? well I'm that nigga who's tired of trying to fit. that nigga, raised in so much white it seeps out of her pores when she least expects it. i'm that canadian, trying to be jamaican, african faking, nigga. That sexual tigress—hardcore exterior chick. The one who wants her clit licked on the regular/bout to go buy a vibrator typa nigga. that creative type writer. singer. actor. Actor who's trying to get paid for what she does in everyday life on the regular. that platinum blond wig-owning, sweet essential oil wearing, bougie, materialistic, spiritual nigga. that one that doesn't fit. that sister outsider wommin spirit blazing fire shy as hell typa sister nigga. that on the prowl saying she's dying to fuck but scared as hell when the time comes kinda sister. who can cum if the loving's good. that eyebrow plucking, armpit shaving, on occasion, hairy-legged sista. the one who fluctuates from style to style, from gender to gender, from sanity to other, sista.

so yeah—all this to say. i've got so much floating in my head and in the recesses of my psyche that i can't even begin to take on anything more than my own tears/fears. selfish. i know. i am. trying to keep it real with me first. i know. i am. interior walls of defense are thick and reinforced with steel. my soul.

it's crazy right. 'cause u know this world has been ruled by male misogynist energy for so long that all the female energy is suspended on the cross and our blood is being shed. with each rape, with each distorted image, with each apology we make for who we are. that female energy, circumcised, manipulated and relegated to the back, so that intellectual debates about black political change can occur. man. my womb is the change. call me that angry black bitch sister nigger. birthing the next generation with no support or voice. suicide. hovers on the breath, in the realms of thought of all the so-called strong, black, women, warriors i know.

is there room in the revolution to deal with that?

send blessings. we need them.

from the cold north,
naila

(Belvett)[3]

**BLACK CULTURAL PRODUCTION** in Canada is often based on the premise that there exists within a Black person an intuitive African connection, aesthetic, and spirituality. Steven Green asserts that Black storytellers in Toronto "are informed by the western world around them—speaking it's [sic] language and influenced by its principles—yet harking back in a spiritual, intuitive way to their ancestral African roots; a tapping into the soul of blackness" (Richardson and Green vii). The reach of this gesture towards an African soul is informative given that many Black artists in Canada come from Caribbean lineages that span multiple generations. Yet, like much of the discourse about Black cultural production in Canada and beyond, this concept of a spiritual and intuitive Africanness bypasses and surpasses the centuries of cultural formation in other places (in this case, the Caribbean) and privileges instead the perceived legacy of an implicitly African influence. I wrote "star" after my first visit to South Africa, which was also my first visit to Africa. My expectations of how it would feel to place my feet on African soil were great. I imagined taking my shoes and socks off, standing barefoot, toes curled deep into the land. I quietly billed the trip a rite of passage, a journey to my homeland.

The lack of specificity embedded in my romantic anticipation of primordial connection with any region of Africa signals the ambiguity of the transatlantic slave trade via The Door of No Return. However, it also forecloses other non-Black ethnicities that may constitute my blood: the Caribs and Arawaks who lived in Jamaica prior to Spanish and British colonial rule, my paternal grandmother Keleta whose name is the same as a river that runs between Ethiopia and Eritrea, my mother Mae whose name means "mother" in Portuguese, my father's last name Belvett which is thought to be Spanish in origin. In my family we have no factual explanations for the progenitors of these names;

instead, they have been crafted as sites of family mythologies that, along with other artefacts, gesture towards multiple ethnicities and nations—none of which suggest any connection with South Africa. I knew this before I got on the plane to Cape Town. I knew this long before I got on planes to Jamaica, the United States, and other countries I have visited with the underlying hope of feeling an ancestral connection and shared context, particularly with those with a similar skin colour. Each of these trips represented a search, a longing for the sense of self-assurance that I thought I would feel if I could only find a place where I unequivocally belonged. Instead, each of my trips fell abysmally short and left me more disappointed than reassured.

Performance expectations of female blackness shifted in each national context as did the performance tools at my disposal. In South Africa, my foreign English elevated my class status in a context where my skin colour and gender were unremarkable. In Jamaica, the pace of my gait and the style of my dress labelled me foreigner and consequently perceived as affluent and gullible. In the United States, my English, gait, dress, gender, and skin colour were barely noticed, while my Canadian nationality labelled me culturally inferior. In those instances, I forwarded my Jamaican ethnicity to attain cultural relevance, particularly in moments when my class status was notably inferior to members of the well-established, multigenerational, African American bourgeoisie. I knew all of this long before I wrote "star" and its content reflects my experiences of inhabiting a body viewed as female and Black in various nations that engender and expect disparate performances of female blackness.[4] I use the word nation here to refer not only to state-legislated geographical borders but also to dominating discourses within colluding and competing Black nationalisms that influence perceptions of female blackness in Canada, particularly those emanating from the United States and the Caribbean.

One of the central challenges that "star" grapples with then is how to adequately articulate expansive nuanced experiences of female blackness in ways that disrupt the violent cultural domination that Black nationalisms so often enact through and on inhabitants of bodies read as female and Black. In "National Culture" Fanon theorizes that, "while at the beginning the native intellectual used to produce his work to be read exclusively by the oppressor, whether with the intention of charming him or of denouncing him through ethnic or subjectivist means, now the native writer progressively takes on the habit of addressing his own people" (Fanon 2006, 120). At the very least, positioning "star" in relation to Fanon in this way is problematic insofar as it suggests that his analysis of male writers includes people like me. However, when read through José Esteban Muñoz's theory of disidentification,[5] Fanon's scholarship can be usefully taken up even by those collapsed by the blind spots of his politics. Fanon's observations about the objectives of native male writers suggest ways to attentively conceptualize how oppression, progress, and audience are defined by writers who inhabit bodies read as female and Black that are routinely gendered and racialized. In "Speaking in Tongues: Dialogics, Dialectics, and the Black Woman Writer's Literary Tradition," Mae Gwendolyn Henderson provides a particularly insightful theorization of African American women writers' use of "multivocality" to articulate counter-narratives on numerous planes: "Black women writers enter into testimonial discourse with Black men as Blacks, with white women as women, and with Black women as Black women. At the same time, they enter into a competitive discourse with Black men as women, with white women as Blacks, and with white men as Black women" (Henderson 20). In this regard, "star" attempts to forego familiar analysis of the systemic inequities that plague the implicitly white status quo and seeks to offer instead a provocative critique of dominating discourses within varied manifestations of Black nationalisms. "star" seeks to interrogate Black nationalisms' historical and contemporary practice of charting female blackness as a geographical nation space.

The central preoccupation of interior analysis and critique in writing by inhabitants of female Black bodies can be productively read as an activist-response to Black nationalisms' divisions of labour and valuation of gendered work. The dominant trend in the Black nationalisms this book queries renders family and community work (overwhelmingly performed by inhabitants of bodies read as female and Black) hyperinvisible and public leadership (overwhelmingly performed by inhabitants of male Black bodies) hypervisible. This patriarchal and classed categorization of work has deep historical roots in Black nationalisms, and it persists within the infrastructures that manufacture the dominating streams of nationalisms in present-day cultures. A consideration of "star" is how to embody, in page performance, the self-reflexivity that personal and lived experience and feminist and postcolonial discourses often assert as necessary for the substantive political engagement of decolonization. That said, though available spaces for attentive articulations and mindful perceptions of female blackness in Canada often appear limited, they are not foreclosed. Here too, Henderson provides a productive theoretical framework called "simultaneity of discourse" that suggests another way to read audiences' and inhabitants' perceptions of sexualized performances of female blackness in "star." Henderson's "simultaneity of discourse" makes clear that critical readings of texts by Black women necessitate an analytical shift towards valuing multiple subjectivities of female blackness and an analytical shift away from an ontology of humanity predicated on the existence of a pure, implicitly white, self. Henderson writes,

> [Simultaneity of discourse] is meant to signify a mode of
> reading which examines the ways in which the perspectives
> of race and gender, and their interrelationships, structure
> the discourse of Black women writers. Such an approach
> is intended to acknowledge and overcome the limitations
> imposed by assumptions of internal identity (homogeneity) and
> the repression of internal differences (heterogeneity) in racial
> and gendered readings of works by Black women writers. (17)

Henderson asserts that our reading of Black women writers be contextualized within a literary criticism where sex and race are co-constituted. As such, it is helpful to consider my performance poem "star" as an exploration of multiple female Black interior and exterior identities. My extension of Henderson's theory of the interior life of Black women writers into that of the external spaces they occupy is an effort to take seriously Patricia Hill Collins's insightful critique of African American feminists of the hip hop generation. In *Black Sexual Politics: African Americans, Gender, and the New Racism*, Collins argues that African American feminists of the hip hop generation politicize personal-identity narrative in popular culture without substantive engagement in the structural social conditions that deeply inform the lives of Black women. "The authors clearly understand and have progressive views on racism, sexism, heterosexism, and class exploitation, but their narratives do not examine the structural foundations of how these systems affect women as well as women's organized responses to them (for example, the women's movement)" (Collins 2006, 188–89). As a member of the hip hop generation influenced by the African American feminisms that Collins analyzes, I flag this as a potential blind spot.

The historical trajectory of female Black life in Canada charts its course roughly from legal objects of property valued specifically for reproductive capabilities, to a contemporary commodification wherein nations assign value in accordance with the sexualization they deem most profitable. "star" identifies these sexualized performances as five overlapping spheres of identity in the line, "call me that angry Black bitch sister nigga." Each performance space contains capacity for engagement with the cultural determinants of gender, race, sexual orientation, and economics espoused by various nationalisms. Black nationalisms have a long history of contention in which various factions have colluded and competed to set a nation's agenda. Fanon's theorization of a "literature of combat" is particularly useful in contemplating how nationalism is a contested space that "calls on the whole people to fight for their existence as a nation. It is a literature of combat, because it moulds the national consciousness, giving it form and contours and flinging open before it new and boundless horizons; it is a literature of combat because it assumes responsibility, and because it is the will to liberty expressed in terms of time and space" (Fanon 2006, 120).

"star" is not a clarion call for the dismantling of all the Black nationalisms that constitute its primary audience. Quite the contrary, "star" implies that Black nationalisms are deep-rooted institutions with important legacies and popular influence. The text suggests that within contemporary articulations of Black nationalisms there are dominating cultures of misogyny that require further interrogation. To this end, "star" asks one central question: "is there room in the revolution to deal with that?" Drawing from Fanon's previously mentioned theorization of native male writers,[6] "star" may be thought to conceptualize *oppression* as spatial ("room"), *progress* as "revolution," and *audience* as those who participate in Black nationalisms. When the text asks, "is there room in the revolution to deal with that?" the "that" it seeks to assert is the vulnerabilities, insecurities, fears, and dreams of inhabitants of bodies read as female and Black who are invested in Black nationalisms. To this end, it is an interior and exterior query of female blackness in relation to Black nationalism.

Another reading of the text emerges when the dual interior-exterior analysis of female Black writing is considered against the framework of Fanon's critique of the bourgeoisie vis à vis nation-building projects. Fanon writes, "The national bourgeoisie turns its back more and more on the interior and on the real facts of its undeveloped country, and tends to look toward the former mother country and the foreign capitalists who count on its obliging compliance" (Fanon 2006, 122). We might also consider how writing by inhabitants of female Black bodies, including "star," grapples with the trappings of what is arguably the new "mother country"—what might be called transnational empire, which is not defined by geographical borders but instead by a loosely-shared cultural and economic exposure and aspirations. Furthermore, within transnational empires, the resources of nations are so thoroughly intertwined that geopolitical autonomy is effectually unattainable even though the rhetoric of nationalism persists as a tool to organize masses of people. To this end, "first world" moves away from a handful of state-legislated geographical locations and instead signals a classed space for all those who benefit from transnational empires. In other words, "first world" signals a transnational class stratum that transcends class definitions within cultural and state-legislated nation spaces. Thus, while Henderson astutely draws our attention to the interplay of sex and race in African American women's writing, I would argue that we must also frame writing by inhabitants of racialized female Black bodies as being in constant conversation with class. "star" grapples with transnational empire by occupying some of the class positions made available to inhabitants of female Black bodies in Canada by various Black nationalisms.

"star" is in conversation with class with its emphasis on material consumption ("a luxury vehicle") that signals affluence in Jamaican, Canadian, and U.S. Black nationalisms. The focus on class continues, "complete with tan leather interior and brown tinted windows (not Black—that's far too ghetto)" (Belvett 2002, 63).This privileging of tan and brown and devaluation of Black connotes the skin politics of colourism which has its roots in British colonial rule whereby skin shade corresponds to class status and social mobility. In the Jamaican context, colourism carries the violent racial legacies of colonization; where lighter skin signals upper-middle class insofar as it suggests the presence of white British ancestry, refinement, humanity, intelligence, etc., while darker skin signals working class by suggesting Black African ancestry, grotesqueness, savagery, a lack of intelligence, etc. These skin politics also undoubtedly inform perceptions of available sexual spaces for those who inhabit female Black bodies in Jamaica and in diasporic Jamaican culture. As Jamaica moves further into independence and further away from overt British colonial rule, increasingly various shades of people occupy class strata that largely would not have been available to them in the past. Yet, there is still no room for black tinted windows in "star"'s luxury vehicle—the prized middle-class possession and symbol of heteronormativity—because black remains "far too ghetto."

Within the spectrum of Black nationalisms that inform this terrain of inquiry (Canadian, Jamaican, and African American), "ghetto" has different meanings. Indeed, they signal extreme poverty as defined by their state-legislated geographical boundaries and they are all symbolized through Black bodies. Arguably, however, in the United States, "ghetto" is also a popular culture hip hop aesthetic and commodity, while in Canada it is also used as an adjective that indicates a momentary slippage in class performance (i.e., "that was so ghetto"). Given its "skin politics," "ghetto" in Jamaica also connotes darker skin and specifically in Jamaican dancehall culture it has been articulated in ways that deeply inform how female blackness is sexualized and thus which performances are available to inhabitants of these bodies.[7] Hope argues that, "Dancehall culture's dialogue of extreme violence and crass, vulgar sexualities disturbs the peace of traditional Jamaica because it represents a viable alternative and a contending power that rivals the dominance of the traditional bourgeois class" (Hope 130). "star's" capacity to separate from the Jamaican bourgeoisie is complicated because regardless of my sex, race, class, sexual orientation, ability, or other cultural signifier, as a Canadian I am a member of the transnational empire. And so, for a Jamaican nation space navigating the underdevelopment that transnational empire requires, Canada, and all those who have access to its spoils, is mythologically and materially collapsed into bourgeois status. As Hope explains, "One should note that a trip abroad ("going to foreign") is a highly prized avenue of social and economic mobility for many Jamaican men and women, particularly those from the inner cities and the lower working classes. An opportunity to visit the United States, England or Canada is perceived as an instant marker of status and economic and social mobility" (Hope 73–74).

Frustration mounts in "star" as it grapples with the constantly shifting spaces that constitute Black nationalisms and the various performances that are necessary to gain entrance and maintain membership within them. "i don't even know if i have the energy to talk politics, discuss world issues, drop names, show how well read (red) i am, be 'deep' as i negotiate my way into a whole other club of the conscious conscious really conscious Black crew" (63). This foreclosure of discussion, not having "the energy" for civic engagement, has embedded within it a multivocality that I had not consciously sought to signal in its composition. The double entendre I meant to reference with my use of "read" and "red" was that the former signals book intelligence, while the latter is a Jamaican expression for being high from marijuana. Performances of both states of read/red hold important currency in all the Black nationalisms that "star" addresses. However, in Jamaican dancehall culture, red has another very specific sexualized meaning that Hope describes: "The redness of the labia denotes a healthy, strong vagina and, by extension, a healthy, strong, aggressive woman whose submission or subjugation is symbolized by the forceful, painful removal and negation of the healthy red of the labia. Hence, [dancehall artiste] Spragga Benz's exhortation to 'dig out di red'" (Hope 49). I grew up hearing those lyrics to Spragga Benz's song "Jack It Up" and so many other explicit, violent dancehall lyrics. I grew up with hip hop and dancehall, both cultures finding expression, invoking sexualizations, and articulating Black nationalisms in the basements, high school gymnasiums, and backyards that housed the parties of my youth in Toronto. Sometimes I would stop dancing in protest to a song I found particularly offensive. Those momentary refusals to perform (in this case, dance) disrupted the relationship between audience and performer in ways that complicate the perceived possibilities and efficacies of *this is who I perform.*

In *Theatre Audiences: A Theory of Production and Reception*, Susan Bennett asserts that an audience makes meaning out of performance in part based on the extent to which they understand themselves to have a shared and similar interpretation of it. Bennett argues that "A crucial aspect of audience involvement, then, is the degree to which a performance is accessible through the codes audiences are accustomed to utilizing, the conventions they are used to recognizing, at a theatrical event" (Bennett 112). A key difference for Black women, drawing from Hurston's analysis, is that everyday life is comparable to being always on stage because dominant society thrusts people at the intersection of blackness and femaleness into a state of *perpetual performance*. Therefore, when a person refuses to embody female blackness in ways that are easily decipherable by an audience, that person momentarily disrupts the audience's expectations and understanding of female blackness—like a stage manager suddenly turning up all the stage and house lights in the middle of a performance. When people read as female and Black refuse to perform familiar acts, others are forced out of the comfortable role of audience member who is permitted, if not expected, to put forth little effort and be entertained. These moments of disruption are fleeting because the pervasive circulation of dominant narratives of female blackness that are steeped in historical tropes and stereotypes means that audiences can and do quickly adjust to these disruptions without necessarily changing the stereotypical, oppressive tropes that inform them. But, nonetheless, these ruptures in expected performances of female blackness do require the audience to, at the very least, pause because the codes and conventions they are accustomed to receiving are momentarily unavailable.

Sometimes I refused to perform/dance to "Jack It Up" and other songs with comparable lyrics because I was a burgeoning woman of the nineties and I wanted to interrupt and mark the misogyny. I listened to African American hip hop artist Queen Latifah and believed Black nationalism meant "Ladies First" like her famous song title and lyrics featuring Monie Love. I also listened to female dancehall artist Tanya Stephens whose song "You nuh ready fi dis yet" chastised men who are inattentive to whether their female sexual partners are satisfied with the encounter and whether they have had an orgasm. In the song, Stephens asks men if they inquire about their sexual partners satisfaction and states plainly that within the context of a heterosexual pairing, sexual intimacy cannot end until the woman says that she is satiated.

So, I folded my arms in protest to the misogynist lyrics at some of those parties. I refused to wine (a way of dancing to reggae music) to some songs. But some nights, between the dancehall and hip hop lyrics of the most popular songs, there was not much music left to dance to and I wanted to dance. I picked my battles. I performed disinterest. No teenage boy was good enough. I refused to dance with them. By the end of the night, I danced with them, but sometimes I wined my body harder. Nothing soft in my burgeoning performances of female blackness. Hope argues that the pervasiveness of androcentrism, patriarchy, and misogyny led to "the rise of the raunchy female artiste" whose diverse lyrical skills are deployed to "either aggressively and demandingly ride the sexual thrust with their own suggestive and raw lyrics and performance, like Lady Saw, or rebuff the attacks on the female body and feminine sexuality with lyrics that derogate male sexual performance, courtship or conquest, like Tanya Stephens and Ce'cile" (Hope 51). Embedded in articulations of autonomy, nuance, and contradictions over and within the sexualized female Black body then are possibilities to disrupt Black nationalisms' violent imaginaries. With its use of explicit sexual language, assertions of multiple class positions and ideological affiliations, "star" extends "the raunchy female artiste" tradition of Tanya Stephens, Lady Saw, and Ce'cile into performance poetry (Hope 50-1). Unfortunately, however, the text only makes modest efforts to disturb the heteronormativity that is so prevalent in the Black nationalisms it seeks to trouble. "star" only gestures towards non-heterosexual orientations with a quote from African American artist Meshell Ndegeocello's song "I'm Diggin You (Like An Old Soul Record)" and a passing comment about fluctuating from "gender to gender."

"star's" veiled and minor engagement with heterosexism is informative given its willingness to explicitly interrogate other

tenets of Black nationalisms' institutionalized cultures of domination. The text's tentative expression of these modest efforts to distort the hegemony of heteronormativity perhaps reflects a larger,
challenging project that Collins identifies in the Black nationalism of the United States. "Of race, class, gender, and sexuality
as systems of oppression, for many people, heterosexism remains
the most difficult to understand and, in many cases, to even see
as being a system of oppression" (Collins 2004, 19). I recognized
heterosexism as a system of oppression when I wrote "star" and
still I failed to engage substantively with the issue. What this
omission underscores is the persistence of heterosexism in each
manifestation of Black nationalism under examination, largely
because heterosexism asserts specific notions of acceptable mod-
els of family and community—and female blackness is routinely
collapsed into those two spaces. Subsequently, any substantive
articulation of the range of sexual orientations that inhabitants
of female Black bodies occupy is perceived as a threat to family
and community that are already under siege by institutionalized
anti-blackness that makes Black life vulnerable. That vulnerability is explored in "star" because thoughts of death sit below the
surface of the bravado of the poem and its performance of the
warrior-like strength so often attributed to those who inhabit female Black bodies in Canada, Jamaica, and the United States.[8]
"star's" reference to suicide[9] is an effort to underscore the urgency
of the calls for equality and social justice within the Black nationalisms that form the communities of those who inhabit female
Black bodies. Whichever sexualized performance is ascribed to
and performed by inhabitants of female Black bodies, the poem's
concluding emphasis on suicide makes clear that the stakes are
high, desires to communicate are great, and frustrations with
the limitations of language and space are palpable. Thus, questions that haunt "star" include: Which dominating sexualized

performances of female blackness are made invisible in the text? Which other dominating streams of thought in Black nationalisms does the text mobilize, trouble, and transgress?

I performed "star" verbatim as a performance poem in South Africa in 2003, but upon my return to Canada I revised it for Canadian audiences into a performance poem entitled "this is my rant." I later further revised the performance poem into a song with the same title. The texts that were deleted from "star"[10] and the ideas emphasized by their removal for performance suggest ways to further understand the sexual and national political contexts that most inform the performance poetry of those who inhabit female Black bodies in contemporary Canada. Had I performed "star" for an African American audience, I anticipate that I would have made some alterations. I would have had to consider how the popular use of the word "nigger" emerges from and is deeply rooted in African American culture. This means that the word's effectiveness as a provocative term in the performance renditions of "star" would have been diminished. As such, I likely would have needed to explore performing the word "nigger" with familiarity, which would have placed more emphasis on the poem's rationale for abandoning other terms like "sister" and "woman." Contemplations of these revisions and omissions gesture towards ways in which inhabitants of female Black bodies perform various fantasies of female blackness depending on the political contexts of the various nations states in which we wish to gain, maintain, and/or foreclose access. Furthermore, it suggests how text is transformed when the audience's reading of the performer as female and Black is foregrounded in performance. On the page, "star" is an embodied text meant to indicate multiple nuances. The performance poem "this is my rant" requires different nuances to be forwarded, particularly given what female blackness connotes and denotes in Canada. In this regard, the transformation of "star" into "this is my rant" is a departure point to contemplate broader conversations not only about conditions of sexualized and nationalized performances of female blackness but also about performance poetry as an effective form of female Black cultural production in Canada.

Within the context of ethnographic studies, D. Soyini Madison describes the translation of fieldwork into performance as a "process of elimination" that is simultaneously about achieving "the goals of the project" and about "trust" (2006, 400). Reading through Madison's methodology, "star" is the source material and "this is my rant" is its live performance. Within this construct, the principal goal of the latter is the portrayal of complex female Black subjectivities to predominantly Black and predominantly non-Black audiences in Canada. At stake in this exchange between performer and audience is the identification of dominant epistemological assertions about female blackness, namely that it is not an actual site of Canadianness. In other words, inhabitants of female Black bodies in Canada must ultimately be from somewhere else—immigrants with some other national identity—despite a history of female blackness that locates us on this soil long before it was nationalized as Canada.[11]

The translation of the source material, "star," into the live performance "this is my rant," underwent a "process of elimination" of text that gestured towards female blackness in geographical locations other than Canada. For example, sections in Jamaican Creole were removed[12] and the critique of famed Jamaican reggae artists was deleted.[13] In addition, female blackness as a Canadian identity was asserted through the elimination of some African American language and cultural references.[14] Furthermore, explicit references to mental illness as a consequence of the systems of oppression at work in the daily lives of inhabitants of bodies read as female and Black in Canada were removed.[15] Madison writes about the process of revisiting notes to identify how the materials relate to one another and how they can be assembled to achieve multiple goals. Madison identifies the following: "relationships of contrast, comparison, extension, and completion for the purpose of persuasion and advocacy as well as relationships of texture, intonation, tone, and lyricism for the purpose of linguistic style and aesthetic imagery" (Madison 401). By virtue of its assertion of my solitary body on stage, "this is my rant" advocates for female blackness as a site of Canadianness; in style and imagery it seeks to complement and contradict ideas evoked by dominant Black and non-Black discourses. Madison argues that "Moving from the field to the [performance] script, it is purpose that energizes will; then, it is politics and beauty that energizes performance" (Madison 401). The overarching politic that comes to light in the analysis of the transformation of "star" into "this is my rant," through Madison's rubric, is the assertion of a nuanced female blackness firmly situated in a Canadian context. Tellingly, "star's" line "i'm that sista nigga" is subtly and substantively revised in "this is my rant" to "call me that sista nigga." In the delicate balance that Madison's reference to "the goals of the project" and "trust," I assessed that it was too risky to ask Black and especially non-Black audiences to consider nuance and irony in a moment when they would simultaneously see a female Black body on stage and hear her say "i'm that sista nigga." While the fixed site of the page permitted "star" to play with "i'm that sista nigga" as an example of *this is who I perform,* the liveness of performance required the words to make audible that which dominant discourse utters inaudibly when people read as female and Black occupy stage space. In this regard, "call me that sista nigga" makes the implicit explicit and indicates to the audience that it is, indeed, a moment of *this is who I perform* and not *this is who I am.*

Another site of female Black cultural production in Canada with modes of meaning-making that differ from those of performance poetry is Black theatre. Some of the artists and plays that are part of the genre in Canada are: trey anthony's *da kink in my hair;* Lisa Codrington's *Cast Iron,* Lorena Gale's *Je Me Souviens*; ahdri zhina mandiela's *who knew grannie: a dub aria*; Amanda Parris's *Other Side of the Game*; Djanet Sears's *The Adventures of a Black Girl in Search of God*; and d'bi.young anitafrika's *blood.claat.* I would argue that Black theatre in Canada is part of a broader transnational movement that Nigel Gibson describes as "emerging from below and working out its ideas in the untidy politics of open discussion and disagreement" (Gibson 114). They are performances that are grounded in the complex conflicts and frictions of Black personal and lived experiences articulated in Canadian frameworks. The following analysis of my play *stuck*[16] focuses on the relationship between body and text to compare performance poetry and theatre as sites of female Black cultural production that facilitate different expressions of *this is who I perform* in Canada.

On three brisk fall nights in Montreal in 2001, dozens of people climbed two flights of steep and narrow stairs, mingled in an eclectically furnished foyer, crossed creaking floors, and entered a black box theatre space to watch my fifty-five-minute solo play/performance piece entitled *stuck*. My description of *stuck* for publicity materials was:

> walking the tight rope of sanity... suicide is not a far cry. the reality of her father's death hits her and she finds herself stuck. splitting into two thousand pieces... she struggles with issues of class, culture, colour, shade, gender, sexuality and love... empty inside she finds herself coping but not dealing. (postcard)

Black Theatre Workshop, infinitheatre, and I billed this workshop production as "performance poetry meets theatre" (postcard). Both the performance poetry and theatre that this research
and writing are concerned with and seek to better understand
are public performances that have historically reaffirmed and
disturbed Black and other communities' perceptions of a singular female Black self in social, political, and cultural contexts.
Mapped out and orchestrated, my body had many stakeholders
during the *stuck* run. It had specific places to be at very specific
times. The technical run had determined how light cues would
wash it, the director ahdri zhina mandiela and I had blocked
it, the set back- and fore-grounded it. I was dressed in the same
clothes each night, too, chosen by the director and me; there was
no costume designer. Canadian theatre traditions suggest that
the extent of my input in these processes was a luxury—perhaps
even slightly subversive.

(Preset lights fade to Black. Lights fade up on bare Black floor.
Naila sings off stage)

(sung) i am so
lonely
though people surround me

(Naila enters downstage centre—bare foot, hair short
(disheveled), clothed in light blue and gray plaid pajamas.
Carries and drags 100m of thick rope onto the worn stage.
She circles space, lets rope trail behind her, delineates
boundaries of play, marks the ring, builds the set.)

my heart still feels
empty

> i am so
> lonely
> (Belvett 2)

Performance poetry conventions suggest that substantial consultation about where to move my body on stage and how to clothe it for performance is absurd. Performance poets clothe, map, chart, and orchestrate our bodies for the stage based on our pre- and of-the-moment assessments of the performance poetry space. In this context, the term "performance poetry space" is used to identify: the performance poet's body, the moments of performance, audience placement, audience temperament, audience composition, event context, personal desires, and professional goals. Furthermore, there is arguably minimal expectation that all the poems performed will communicate a central narrative or any overtly linear or cohesive narrative at all. As such, the performance poet's body functions then as theatre's equivalent to a central narrative, the play setting, and the world of the play. This positions the body as subtext to the performance. As Rachael Van Fossen, then Artistic Director of Black Theatre Workshop, observed when I interviewed her about the performance of *stuck*,

> there are moments when it's more identifiably Naila and sort of moving in and out of or oscillating between: we clearly see Naila in a personal context in a concrete space (on the phone, talking to a friend) and then times when [Naila] is not in a real space that we can identify that concretely and then it feels more like it has oscillated back to performance poetry.

This lack of "real space" is in fact the real space of performance poetry—the body on stage is there in front of the audience in real time; thus, it becomes the central narrative, setting, and/or world constructed. Furthermore, the use of body as the constant, real setting is integral to performance poetry's capacity to engage, provoke, and interact with audiences. Victoria Stanton and Vincent Tinguely's *Impure: Reinventing the Word: The Theory, practice, and Oral History of 'Spoken Word' in Montreal* and T.L. Cowan's edited special issue called "Spoken Word Performance" in the *Canadian Theatre Review* both provide insights into how spoken word, and performance poetry in general, theorize and occupy performance space.

In "Gestures of the Dancing Voice: Reloading the Can(n)on under the Influence of Dub," Klyde Broox asserts that as performance poets, "dubpoets treat the stage like a page and, in performance, body becomes subtext that should be read as such" (Broox 78). This autonomy of body in performance affords performance poets considerable power in determining how we will present ourselves to the audience. However, performance poets are certainly not exempt from the historical, social, political, and cultural constructs assigned to their bodies based on where and when they perform and to whom. As a performance poet I have substantial autonomy over the placement and dress of my body within performance poetry spaces, whereas in Canadian theatre the actor's body is often scripted by the playwright, clothed by the costume designer, and moved about by the director. I focus here on the actor as equivalent to the performance poet because, ultimately, they are the ones on stage. However, using the lexicon of theatre, the performance poet is like a solo performer.

Text was the cause of much anxiety for me in the writing and performances of *stuck*. To fulfill its billing as a workshop production and meet theatre audiences' expectations, I was expected by the director, artistic director, and me to write fifty-five to sixty minutes of performance-worthy material. The set length of performance poetry at the time ranged from eight to fifteen minutes and rarely more than thirty minutes. I recall the pressures of being, at the time, primarily a performance poet writing in a theatre context where page count mattered and my ability to produce pages seemed akin to my ability to qualify as a legitimate playwright. Once the text was produced and finalized, it, like my body, was mapped and orchestrated. The lighting cues were determined by it and depended on it; the blocking was sourced from it; I constructed the set each night in timing with it. The text had a specific order, and my consistent reproduction of that order was of critical importance to the convention of a Canadian theatre run. This convention necessitated a consistent reproduction of the finalized text.

This privileging of text and textual order in theatre in Canada is radically different from the way text is often used in performance poetry in Canada. In the case of performance poetry, it may be useful to think of text as subtext where the privileged text is performance poetry space. During the process of writing *stuck*, I was not particularly preoccupied with how I would represent the text on the page. I had not come from a theatre-trained background and *stuck* was the second play that I had both written and performed. I now know that there are key differences in how performance is represented as text on the page in theatre, and how text stores performance on the page in performance poetry. In the latter, text is not meant to embody the performance on the stage; thus, the emphasis is not on its ability to represent the performance as envisioned by the performance poet. Therefore, when performance poetry is captured on the page for performance, there is often no need to use playwriting conventions such as stage directions or even punctuation marks as cues to producers, dramaturgs, directors, or actors. Broox argues that "Dubpoets see poems as instruments, not ornaments. We use speech, gesture, music, song, dance, and even sound effects to stylize vernacular language and perform memorable narratives for audiences" (Broox 78).

In the case of the textual version of *stuck*, performance poetry's relationship with text trumped that of theatre. Van Fossen noted, "it was difficult for me to read the text and grasp it and follow it … it was certainly more challenging to grasp quickly then a linear play that follows an Aristotelian cause and effect narrative." Furthermore, not only is the text of a performance poem not intended to represent the performance; in performance poetry, the text also often changes, shifts, and evolves in performance poetry space. In addition, during a performance, decisions about which texts to perform and the order in which to perform them changes, shifts and evolves based on the poet's assessments of performance poetry space—namely what is at stake between the performer and their audience. In "Shards of Light," Adeena Karasick asserts, "you have to change the text, make these alterations, nip/tucks to fit the moment" (bissett and Karasick 19). Textual representation in performance poetry is secondary to performance and not necessarily indicative of the performance poet's vision of the performance. As Van Fossen notes, "it was a form that was very new to me in terms of the writing itself and the rhythms of it … it did and does come alive in the performance of it … so seeing even that first workshop production [of *stuck*] was a very very [sic] strong experience for me even as rough as it was." A performance poet can emphasize what d'bi.young anitafrika (then known as debbie young) called the "doing" of the text in performance. "When I'm writing, I see myself performing it. So I don't see the poetry on paper, I see it onstage. In my head I see myself doing, *doing* the poem. It's very clear to me, clear as day" (Stanton and Tinguely 65). Performance poets can store text on the page and/or adjust text in the moment to facilitate the "doing" that they envision is necessary in performance poetry space (Stanton and Tinguely 65). Furthermore, as Nasser Hussain observes in "Consuming Language: Embodiment in the Performance Poetry of bpNichol and Steve McCaffery," "the audience is implicated in the social construction of meaning: rather than gazing at the painting, we are witnesses to and conspirators in its creation" (Hussain 20).

On closing night, my mother, sister, and five cousins drove to Montreal from Toronto and New York to attend *stuck*. I was petrified. Yes, *stuck* charts my grieving process after the death of my father, but it also—with varying degrees of autobiographical accuracy—delves into strained familial relationships, mental illness, marijuana use, and forced hospitalizations. I was terrified because the text of the play was cemented and fixed in theatre convention. I remember performing and feeling trapped by my words and their impact on my family members, by my fears of the career repercussions of changing text and breaking theatre form, and by my personal desire to exploit my power of occupying official stage space.[17] I reworded, deleted, and inserted as much text as I could without severely compromising lighting cues and running time. For a moment I broke text, blocking, and theatrical form of playing a memory of myself and instead privileged performance poetry form as I spoke as myself. I produced body and text as performance poetry; "I can't do this anymore," I said. And then I reinserted my body and text back into theatre's order and sang the next scripted song:

> brown girl in the ring[18]
> tra la la la la
> brown girl in the ring
> tra la la la la la
> brown girl in the ring
> tra la la la la
> she looks like a
> (Belvett 6)

Each verse of this children's Jamaican song and game ends with a variation of the line "She looks like sugar in a plum." This song and game are meant to show the prowess of the dancer in the ring, but in *stuck,* my body and text make five unsuccessful attempts to sing the last line of the song. It is always interrupted after, "she looks like a." Three times the interruptions come from taunting voices of implicitly non-Black children making fun of my skin texture and colour; another time it is the sound of bullets fired by four white male police officers at a Black man; in the last instance I interrupt myself and say, "she looks like—she's disappearing." These interruptions are meant to underscore that an implicitly Black Jamaican song celebrating the skill of dancing is truncated when imported into an implicitly white Canadian reality where what the brown girl looks like takes precedence over any skill she might have. After the song is sung, the following text is spoken:

> make me like the other little girls
> lord please.
> just make me like the other little girls,
> with nice skin
> smooth soft skin
> nice skin
> nice light skin
> nice skin
> snow white skin
> lord please.
> pretty please.
> amen.
>
> p.s.
> i promise i'll be really really really
> good.

amen.

again.

sigh
sleep
shame
next morning
skin looks the same. (Belvett 6)

In Black performance poetry in Canada—where body and text often function as subtexts—agency arguably shifts in favour of the person on stage who has more power over the vantage point of their body and who has immediate agency over which texts to use to interrogate what it means to be "dispossessed." Within that context, the performer can shift their body and text to serve and shape performance poetry space. In the meeting of performance poetry and theatre that *stuck* sought to negotiate, theatre's conventions of body and text embodied and inscribed itself onto and into the production. As Van Fossen observes, "[the] experience of seeing it performed, following the story, following the character's journey—absolutely it was theatre, it was very exciting theatre."

*stuck* was subsequently remounted in 2002 at the Summerworks Theatre Festival, in 2003 as a Black Theatre Workshop main-stage production, and at the AfriCanadian Playwrights Festival the same year. With each remounting, the text was moderately changed, and theatre conventions increasingly moved to the fore-ground, the role was acted by another actor, theatrical production values increased, and I became the Assistant Director. "It was clearly much more polished in its production," Van Fossen observed, "it was also very strong theatre—unqualified—yes this is theatre." It was not the embodied performance poetry that "this is my rant" demonstrates, nor the embodied text on a page that "star" navigates. *stuck* sought to negotiate a dynamic meeting place between performance poetry and theatre, but that was clearly trumped by the latter's institutional traditions. This is in large part because unlike performance poetry in Canada, Canadian theatre has been institutionalized through more than seventy years of public funding and decades of substantive academic inquiry.

## An excerpt from my play *What We Deserve*[19]

........................................................................

UMZANSTI    How many paragraphs did she write?

SUNIFYA    Seven.

77    Wow.

UMZANSTI    So many words.

Too many words.

Read it… please.

SUNIFYA    I already read it once and that was more than enough. I'm not giving it any more energy.

77    (*Gestures for* SUNIFYA'S *device*) Pass it here.

SUNIFYA    There's no point. It's from an older white woman and it's basically just a generic example of how white supremacy and anti-Black racism continue to live on in white feminist movements especially in the ways that white women talk to Black women. I'm over it.

77          We'll read it. (SUNIFYA *looks on unimpressed*.) Ok,
            not word for word, just a summary. Oh, paragraph 1
            is definitely a set up. She leads all cordial and
            complimentary, "You … You … So much potential
            … You!"

UMZANSTI    Oh, she put an exclamation mark on that last one.

77          (*To* SUNIFYA) I don't know, friend, it was a good
            speech but definitely not your best delivery. Like,
            not at all.

SUNIFYA     I know, right?

UMZANSTI    (*Reading from the message*) Ooohhh paragraph 2 is
            very passive aggressive. It's so good. It's all, "Me …
            Me … What about me? Talk about me. Talk about
            women like me."

SUNIFYA     Merciful Fadda. (*To* UMZANSTI *in jest*) Why mi
            neva talk 'bout di older white feminist dem? Wha
            happen to mi? Mi nuh know say mi mus always
            talk 'bout dem?

            (*Steups teeth—a Caribbean vocal sound*)

UMZANSTI    I'm lost, yo. We just heard your speech. You talked
            about a bunch of different women … Alice Eagly
            … Ericka Hart … Arundhati Roy, Warsan Shire.
            Who else? Hillary Clinton.

UMZANSTI AND 77
> That's what did it.

UMZANSTI       Yup. Absolutely.

> And even though you didn't mention Hillary's
> "super predators" thing … you did go in on her
> in your speech tonight and not everyone cyan
> manage dem deh truths deh.

> (*Flash back to* SUNIFYA *delivering her speech the
> night before*)

SUNIFYA       In 2008, when Clinton suspended her campaign to
> be the Democratic Party's presidential candidate
> she also spoke about the highest, hardest, glass
> ceiling and told her supporters that because of
> them it had "about 18 million cracks in it" ("Text
> of Clinton"). Discussions about women and
> leadership often include some reference to the
> "glass ceiling," a transparent, omnipresent barrier
> that women have not created and yet are tasked
> with shattering. The glass ceiling metaphor is
> simple and preposterous. It implies that women
> are busy working away and advancing our careers
> by making thoughtful, strategic professional
> choices. And then, suddenly, out of nowhere we
> smash our heads against tempered glass that had,
> unbeknownst to us, been there all along. Are we
> to believe that generations of women just haven't

been smart enough to notice this glass ceiling? Are we to believe that the same women who were savvy and competent enough to get to the ceiling suddenly forgot to assess the challenges ahead? Absolutely not. Women know the challenges we face well. Women have ample personal, anecdotal, and collective evidence of the ways in which systems of oppression work in tandem to keep leadership opportunities just out of our reach.

UMZANSTI    Yup. That's definitely what did your secret admirer in.

SUNIFYA     She's not my secret admirer.

UMZANSTI    (*Laughing*) Oh, but she is, Sunifya, she most certainly is, and she is furious … oh, and in such a good low-key passive aggressive way. (*Reading the message*) "You owe me!"

Um hm. (*Melodramatically to* SUNIFYA) Did you know that?

(*Reads more of the message*) Sunifya, girl, have you given white feminists their respect? (*Bursts out laughing*)

Wow. I mean just think about all the freedom that white women have given you and all you do is talk about women of colour all night long.

77         Yo, this woman really wants you to stay in
whatever tiny box she thinks you would have been
in (*melodramatically and sarcastically*) were it not
for her and her awesome women friends who gave
you and people like you a voice.

        (*Melodramatically and sarcastically*) You think it's
been tough for you Sunifya? Huh? Just imagine
what it would have been like if progressive liberal
white women like her hadn't fought for you!

UMZANSTI     And what do you do with all that they have
given you? You give a speech that made her
feel uncomfortable. Imagine, the experiences
of a successful white middle-aged woman were
decentred at a women's event? Imagine that.
For the entire duration of your speech the most
financially secure, institutionally powerful, racially
privileged demographic of women in the world
were not centred.

        (*Reading melodramatically from the message*)
"You said things I didn't want to hear."

77         But wait. She neva did deh a di university campus
tonight and hear di oomaan introduce me and call
me professor and say dem invite me fi give one
speech? Ah nah dat me did suppose fi do? Mek
di people dem tink? What did she imagine would
happen?

        No, for real. What did she imagine would happen?

UMZANSTI    Were you supposed to stand in a cage and spin around on demand?

77    Was she expecting to see parts of your body on display in bottles of formaldehyde?

    Those days are over.

UMZANSTI    Those days are done.

SUNIFYA    I'll tell her she missed her chance.

(40–41)

# 4

## SILENCE

**THIS CHAPTER CONSIDERS** how silence can be read as a literary device in Dionne Brand's *At the Full and Change of the Moon* and how the physical violence of slavery transforms into a psychic experience for her characters that is felt across generations. In the novel, Brand writes experiences of female blackness that mark generations and transcend the living and the dead. Brand's exploration of multiple generations of Black people from chattel slavery to contemporary times makes visible how *this is who I perform* can be used to respond to how racism so often collapses the details of individual lives. *At the Full and Change of the Moon* is a genealogical collage that begins with the inner narrative of an enslaved woman named Marie Ursule as she attempts to summon her body into motion on a dark early morning of a changing moon in 1824. Her morning's task, as Queen and mastermind of the secret Convoi Sans Peur (Regiment Without Fear), is to serve the lethal Carib poison *woorara* to the eighteen other enslaved people that comprise the forced labour population at de Lambert's Mon Chagrin estate in Trinidad. Just five years earlier, the secretly organized Convoi Sans Peur and their comrades from neighbouring plantations, the Macaque Regiment and Mon Repos Regiment, planned a mass suicide of all the enslaved people. When their plot was discovered, the punishments were barbaric. Marie Ursule was sentenced to thirty-nine lashes, two years with her leg in a ten-pound iron ring, and was fed her own ear. Others were sentenced to life with an iron ring on their leg and others executed. Marie Ursule deploys performances of translucency—of being seen by her dominators and not seen, of knowing herself as human in the face of inhuman treatment.

After the original plot by the regiments of the three neighbouring plantations is discovered and its members brutally punished, Marie Ursule meticulously conceived of a new plan that she decided to wait to execute "until after they took off the ring and after she looked like her mind was repentant and even after that" (Brand 13). She waited five years that were rife with coerced performances of yielding to domination.[1] In this regard, Marie Ursule is part of the violent historical colonial practice of forced performances of female blackness discussed in "Transclucency" of which Sarah Baartman, the so-called "Venus Hottentot," is a prime example. However, like the portrayal of Baartman in Suzan Lori Parks's play *Venus* (where Baartman exhibits agency that problematizes a simplified notion of her in captivity), Marie Ursule performs inhuman subordination without believing herself to be subordinate. Instead, while enacting coerced performances of *this is who I am* (obedient enslaved woman), she plotted, waited, and successfully executed a mass suicide in an unequivocal act of resistance, inner direction, and imagination. Her new plan included two arrangements to which the Convoi Sans Peur's consent is unclear: her daughter Bola would be brought to freedom by her lover, Kamena (a Black man who successfully ran away from the plantation), and she, Marie Ursule, would not kill herself with the others. She decides to remain alive because "[s]he wanted to see the faces of de Lambert and the rest when they discovered her. She wanted to vow to them that it was she, Marie Ursule, who had devastated them" (Brand 18). Marie Ursule's subsequent week-long punishment is vicious. She is beaten until her arms lay limp in their sockets and her face is unrecognizable. She is hung and she is burned. Yet throughout this brutal treatment she repeats, "'This is but a drink of water,' she told them when they killed her. 'This is but a drink of water,' they heard her say after they broke her arms dragging her. After they put the rope around her neck, after she confessed gladly to her own name alone, 'This is but a drink of water to what I have already suffered'" (Brand 21). Marie Ursule's concise refrain encourages the reader to imagine the depth and breadth of devastation that slavery has wrought.

Throughout *At the Full and Change of the Moon*, Brand uses words succinctly to engage the reader's imagination specifically when describing characters' experiences of the violence of the transatlantic slave trade or its violent impact on their lives generations later. I read this as a powerful and effective use of silence. A Trinidadian-born-and-raised writer, Brand crafts the novel as a découpage of prose, letters, and history held together by an acutely poetic narrative—a structure of fiction that is characteristic of Caribbean women's writing (Davies and Fido 4–5). She describes poetry as her "first language" (Abbas) and what binds the narrative collage of the novel together is her expansive poetic sensibility, notably with regards to rhythm, character development, description, and orality. In "Poetry Is Not A Luxury," Audre Lorde asserts that poetry as illumination names ideas that were otherwise "nameless and formless, about to be birthed, but already felt" (Lorde 36).[2] Lorde teaches us, then, that poetry is the act of fashioning words where there were once only feelings. In *The Power of Silence: Social and Pragmatic Perspectives*, Adam Jaworski describes poetry as a "very powerful" form specifically because of "what is left unsaid" (Jaworski 143). In this regard, Brand's poetic narrative emphasizes silence and consequently privileges the attentive reader with information unavailable to the characters because it was lost in slavery. Unable to draw genealogical lines that trace their roots and make visible their shared lineage, many of the characters are relatives in *At the Full and Change of the Moon*; unknowingly, first cousins marry each other and pass one another on the street. To be clear, Brand's use of silence to treat the vestiges of the transatlantic slave trade is not silence as absence; quite the contrary, the transatlantic slave trade and its attendant horrors loom large, a backdrop that silently sets out the lives of Marie Ursule's progenies in the centuries that follow her death. Additionally, Brand's articulation of Marie Ursule's suffering during slavery is visceral and offers readers the possibility to imagine Black life on a continuum from chattel slavery to colonization, to the present.

The violent details of characters' stories that Brand's use of silence suggests, without explicitly naming, can be read as indicative of the impossibility of the English language to fully describe Black life, in large part because the language itself has been used to actively deny Black life. The impossibility of colonial languages is explored by M. NourbeSe Philip in *Zong!* through her unconventional spacing of text on the page to create space to imagine the lives and perspectives of Black people. Kate Siklosi posits that Philip's unorthodox use of text "provide[s] a way of poetically recovering the living silences within the lacunae of historical language" while Kyle Kinaschuk asserts that the breaks in text be read "as silent noises, aquatic and sonic waves, that are extra-linguistically plentiful with sound and movement themselves" (Kinaschuk 54). I have experimented with adding blank spaces, without stage directions, to my play *What We Deserve* and sought to use those spaces, or moments of silence, to create "time within the scripted text for practitioners and audience members to explore their own imaginations without the precision of text as a guide" (Keleta-Mae 2020, 39). In *The Dark Side of the Nation*,

Himani Bannerji describes silence as "highly telling" with meanings that range from "complicity to resistance" (Bannerji 153). In the case of literature, then, the use of silence as a communicative device is determined by the author and the onus of understanding the various meanings rests on the reader. I would argue that, likewise, in the context of *perpetual performance,* the extent to which silence is used in *this is who I perform* is determined by the inhabitant of the body read as female and Black and the onus of making meaning from her silence is on the audience member.

In *Mama's Baby, Papa's Maybe: An American Grammar Book,* Hortense Spillers contemplates contemporary impacts of the transatlantic slave trade and productively posits that the marks of psychic and physical legacies are "hidden to the cultural seeing by skin color. We might well ask if this phenomenon of marking and branding actually 'transfers' from one generation to another, finding its various *symbolic substitutions* in an efficacy of meanings that repeat the initiating moments" (Spillers 67). I read Spillers's theory as an ontology of blackness that begins with the "initiating moments" of the violent conditions of captivity in chattel slavery and continues in future generations because violence is traceable through the materiality of flesh. For those, like me, who are descendants of enslaved people and who are without precise genealogical ties to Africa, Spillers's theory of "transfers" addresses both the dull, persistent ache for a history where the transatlantic slave trade never occurred and our investments in the transformative possibilities of the present and future. To this end, Spillers relieves some of the agony of not knowing our precise lineage through her assurance that our—at times debilitating—fears about threats of violence have context and merit.

Though Spillers posits that the transfer of "marking and branding" is symbolic, she offers no assuaging suggestion that it dissipates in impact over generations. Instead, she plainly states that the meanings transferred are the same as those communicated in the "initiating moments" and are reproduced with equal force across future generations. I find the implications of Spillers's ontological track deeply disturbing, largely because they offer an accurate analysis of my creative writing, personal experience, and lived experience of female blackness in Canada. The cut of the whip thirty-nine times across Marie Ursule's skin, the pain of the ten-pound iron ring on her leg for two years, and the revulsion of being fed her own ear are palpable almost two centuries later. Temporally unfounded fears of surveillance and incarceration undergird my artistic and academic efforts. The perceived risks of participating in robust advocacy for social justice increase exponentially whenever I consider how easy it would be for me to disappear into the institutional abyss of the penal or mental illness systems in Canada. These psychic modes of discipline are further enforced by the persecution of known and unknown female Black social justice activists who have been held in physical captivity. To this end, Spillers's assertion that the markings are not invisible but hidden to "cultural seeing by skin color" resonates profoundly and can also be extended to include cultural seeing by gender. The meanings encoded in the brutal markings on female Black bodies like Marie Ursule's, besieged by the transatlantic slave trade, are transferred to future generations, and form the backdrop of contemporary thoughts and actions.

The silent threat of racist, sexist surveillance in Canada is perceptible. Robyn Maynard's *Policing Black Lives: State Violence in Canada from Slavery to the Present* and Simone Browne's *Dark Matters: On the Surveillance of Blackness* both trace histories of the surveillance of Black people—the geographical focus of the latter is Canada and that of the former is the United States. This threat informs the conditions that demand *perpetual performance* and the unofficial audience for whom inhabitants of bodies read as female and Black are expected to perform in everyday life. For an inhabitant of a body read as female and Black in Canada, the assertion of *this is who I perform* facilitates a conceptual shift from the threat of surveillance to the existence of an invisible audience. In my personal experience, not only does the subtle shift from surveillance to audience facilitate survival in challenging situations, it also powerfully locates performance as a meaningful mode of resistance.

The resistance I write of here is akin to Chela Sandoval's description in "Revolutionary Force: Connecting Desire to Reality." Sandoval asserts that, "[r]esistance is the unspecified term that lies outside the binary configuration of domination and subordination—yet [this] form of resistance is only effective insofar as it is specifically related to the forms of domination and subordination that are currently in place" (Sandoval 161). Thus, the resistance deployed in the conceptual transformation of the presence of surveillance to that of an audience able to thwart the dominator-subordinated binary because the very act of resistance is grounded in the binary's performative quality.[3] My proposed shift to *this is who I perform* from *this is who I am* is an act of resistance. Similarly, *this is who I perform* (as an inner declaration that imagines the female blackness of one's body as a performance) can subvert outside forces' attempts to direct female blackness because the very act of inner direction is grounded in the dynamics of the dominator-subordinated binary.

My theory of *this is who I perform* does not seek to be an ahistorical act void of any vestiges or enactments of oppression, instead it is a strategic contemporary response, an effort to make and claim inhabitable space for those in bodies read as female and Black. In back-to-back chapters of *At the Full and Change of the Moon*, Brand juxtaposes contemporary life with and without performance through the inner narratives of two of Marie

Ursule's great-great-granddaughters, Maya in Amsterdam, and
Eula in Toronto. Maya is born in Curaçao in 1952 and leaves
soon after her union-organizing father is violently murdered by
those opposing his activist efforts. Armed with the money her
father put aside for her to study nursing, Maya heads to Biljmer,
Amsterdam, where her childhood friend Rita gets her a job as
a nurse trainee in a hospital. By the end of the week, Maya determines that the profession repulses her. Drifting about on the
streets of Biljmer one day, she spots a series of women, each in her
own window, each set in a casual scene, each a sex trade worker.
Drawn by the domesticity of their tableaux, Maya changes pro-
fessions and gets a window of her own: "She had arrived at the
window oddly thinking that it was the most ordinary place in the
world. A place to look in and look out. A simple transparent place,
a place to see and to be seen and therefore a place where compli-
cations were clear and strangely plain" (Brand 208). Maya's performances, framed by the window, are not so much an escape from
life but a means to clarify it. The gilded window is an explicit stage
where Maya is the solo performer. Her set designs tend to feature a
straight back chair, a table, and a pack of cards, and her costumes
range from a half-slip to jeans and a merino, to a plastic lizard
head. Her performances are often casual, self-absorbed meditations: watching the movement of light through the windowpane
onto her skin, drinking beer, braiding her hair, reading a book, or
contemplating the half-moon shape of her fingernail beds.

   In "Excess Flesh: Black Women Performing Hypervisibility,"
Nicole Fleetwood examines subversive possibilities in the visual
art, media art, performance art, rap music, and pop music of female Black cultural producers. Fleetwood's study contemplates
what she calls, "an enactment of the gaze that does not necessarily attempt to heal or redress the naked, exploited, denigrated
Black female body tethered to the black imago but understands

the function of this figuration in dominant visual culture. This productive look lays bare the symbols and meanings of this weighted figure" (Fleetwood 111). Though Maya is not a trained artist overtly engaged in the nuanced representation of female blackness in the public artistic sphere, like Fleetwood's subjects, Maya nonetheless displays a sophisticated awareness and unapologetic manipulation of the connotations of her female blackness to her employer and clientele. Maya thinks about the window when she is not there. She tones her body, oils, and suns her skin, and anticipates the next time she will be onstage, framed by the window. Maya's personal and lived experience of life in the window provides important insight into *this is who I perform* as a strategy for inhabitants of female Black bodies. Not only does the window frame Maya, it also frames her audience: "the lookers outside standing in front of cars, or walking by, glancing at her," those who are "shaped" by the glass window (Brand 208). Maya thoughtfully contemplates how to manage the lookers. She experiments with making them feel comfortable and observes that that makes her uncomfortable and so she stops. When she tries turning her back to the lookers, her pimp, Walter, is furious until it becomes evident that her withdrawal draws more customers in. Walter makes several attempts to tell Maya what to do in the window. She ignores him and successfully directs her own performances which, often feature her concentrating on her own thoughts and looking up only if she happens to.

Fleetwood importantly asserts that "the Black female body does not have the same social, economic, and cultural meaning in different locations and times" (Fleetwood 119). An example of this is Maya's first cousin Eula who was born in Trinidad in 1957 and left for Toronto in her early twenties to live with Sese, one of her older sisters who migrated before her. Within two years of her arrival in Canada, Eula gives birth to a baby girl whom she sends home to her mother, nameless prior to moving out of Sese's home. Like her cousin Maya, Eula considers becoming a sex trade worker but decides that she is not quick-witted enough for the profession. Instead, Eula works in a post office and collects old and new maps to create a sense of stability amid a city she describes as "the end of the world," "crumbling with newness, rubbled in glitter" (Brand 238). A place "where everyone has been swept up, all of it, all of us are debris, things that a land cleaning itself spits up" (Fleetwood 238). Eula simultaneously longs for a historical context that gives her moorings and an exhilarating relationship with the present moment to make her feel alive. She determines that neither is possible for her in Canada—the national stage of her existence. An impromptu, harried road trip to Florida makes clear to Eula that the moorings she seeks do not exist in the United States either. She slowly withdraws from family, from friends, and from life. Eula's withdrawal signals a refusal to perform female blackness in Canada despite the *perpetual performance* dominant culture demands of her female blackness. Thus, Eula's personal experience, lived experience, and writing (as evidenced by a letter to her dead mother) can be read as a refusal of *this is who I perform* which offers productive insights into the choice to relate to one's female blackness in Canada as *this is who I am*. Though it is important to note that Eula also at times moves towards *this is who I perform* thus illustrating the challenge of living in a state of *perpetual performance* when one does not always want to perform.

*This is who I perform*, and *this is who I am* are two locations on a continuum of possible responses to the experience of inhabiting a body read as female and Black in Canada. I name and contrast these two sites of theory and praxis to perceive and conceive of their limitations and possibilities. Both epistemological modes overlap, blur, and leak one into the other arguably because they have in common the slippery concept of the existence of "I" that Minh-ha asserts "is, therefore, not a unified subject, a fixed identity, or that solid mass covered with layers of superficialities one has gradually to peel off before one can see its true face. 'I' is, itself, *infinite layers*" (94). My personal experience, lived experience, and creative writing have taught me that *this is who I perform* provides me with more conceptual and imaginative space for my female Black body than *this is who I am* insofar as I can refuse to perform and refuse to attempt to fully be myself in oppressive spaces. Certainly, it is not the same for everyone who identifies as female and Black. And while I inhabit one of the bodies that I am theorizing, it does not preclude me from reproducing the violent colonial and postcolonial act of attempting to contain and regulate female blackness. *This is who I am,* and *this is who I perform* are both appropriate and viable responses to the imposition of *perpetual performance* on inhabitants of female Black bodies in Canada and they are responses that, along with others, can exist within the same person. Brand's character Eula survives. She makes bold choices—she stays in Toronto, does not act on suicidal thoughts, never enquires about her child, and writes, "I would never be in my body as if it were me" (Brand 250).

In "The Black Performer and the Performance of Blackness," Harry J. Elam Jr. examines how William Wells Brown and Charles Gordone use body and language in their respective plays *The Escape; or, A Leap for Freedom* and *No Place to Be Somebody.* Significantly, Elam Jr.'s analysis concludes that these two Black male writers "destabilize the visible" (Elam Jr. 302–3) meanings of blackness using Black male performers' bodies and the words they speak aloud on stage. In *At the Full and Change of the Moon,* Eula works hard to make herself invisible in public, while Maya and Marie Ursule choose hypervisibility in public. Interestingly, however, none of the three women say many words out loud in public. Readers only hear Eula's voice as retold and remembered by her brother Carlyle when he threatens her into driving from Toronto to Florida with his wife to pick him up near the Immigration and Naturalization Service detainee camp that he fled. He says she screamed, "Fuck you, Carlyle!" when he got into the car with his friend. Similarly, readers only hear Maya's voice in a moment of distress when her pimp, Walter, threatens her with a knife at work. She screams "Fok bo, abusado!" and "Sinbergwensa! Mariku!" as Walter crashes through her window, blood runs down her arm, and one of her co-workers tells her to run. In public, Marie Ursule's voice is heard the most of the three women. Her readers hear her haunting refrain "This is but a drink of water to what I have already suffered" (Brand 21) and on occasions prior to the first failed insurrection she tells those who have attempted to own her: "Pain c'est viande beque, vin c'est sang beque, nous va mange pain beque nous va boir sang beque."

Eula, Maya, and Marie Ursule form a striking contrast when their use of private speech to destabilize the visibility of race and gender is examined. Despite their relatively limited public speech, the language of their private inner monologues is vivid and constantly disrupts notions of permissible modes of female blackness. Their unspoken assessments of their circumstances, limitations, and possibilities are astute and their conclusion that words spoken aloud are of little use warrants further analysis. Eula, Maya, and Marie Ursule are not only charged with the work of "destabiliz[ing] the visible" constraints of blackness (Elam Jr. 302–3), but they must also navigate the parameters of *female* blackness. Within this context, the visibility of the body and space available for language spoken in public differ from those who are socially read as male and Black. Eula's *this is who I am* is made possible by combining a reduction in the visibility of the corporeal along with a minimal use of words in public space. Maya's rehearsal of *this is who I perform* is realized through the hypervisibility of the gilded window coupled with public speech that is incoherent to those around her, though overall she is not much more vocal than Eula. Interestingly, Marie Ursule shifts most explicitly between *this is who I am* and *this is who I perform*—she is invisible and says little while plotting the mass suicide and chooses visibility[4] and rehearsed public speech once the rebellion succeeds. I would argue that Marie Ursule's ability to shift effectively between *this is who I am* to *this is who I perform* is enhanced by the overtly violent context of her oppression. Her great-great-granddaughters Eula and Maya are in far more ambiguous contexts at the close of the twenty-first century. They are not formally enslaved, but as Hortense Spillers posits, the violence that Marie Ursule endured "transfers" to Eula and Maya's generation (Spillers 67), such that their personal and lived experiences do not permit them to perceive themselves as free. The visceral psychological transmission of these experiences, coupled with colonialism's ability to reproduce itself (McClintock, Anghie) and the ongoing threat of surveillance, imposes the conditions of *perpetual performance* that demand that people read as female and Black perform dominant culture's fantasies. There is a wide spectrum of responses to the imposition of *perpetual performance*, including *this is who I perform*, and *this is who I am*, and as an inhabitant of a body read as female and Black in Canada I have and will continue to navigate everyday life with performances that draw from that spectrum.

My contemplation of silence as a means of communication stems from a deeper preoccupation with questions of what constitutes permissible speech for inhabitants of bodies read as female and Black and the worldviews we evoke in our writings. I am curious about what we, as writers, silence and how we communicate in silence, particularly at a time in North America when the boundaries of permissible public speech for Black people in

Canada are arguably wider than they have been in centuries. It is within this context of a seemingly open society, where cultural signifiers like race, class, gender, sexual orientation, and ability are discussed in dominant discourse, that the choice of silence becomes arguably more telling. With so much being said, written, photographed, filmed, and sung, the question that emerges is, why are female Black writers using silence as a form of communication for their characters who are female and Black?

The pitfalls of my research and writing about silence seem numerous. I am concerned that what I perceive as its philosophical elements and candid subjectivity will obfuscate readings of its material possibilities and applications. Yet I cannot seem to escape the desire to touch and perhaps even hold an understanding of why silence has been and remains an integral part of my creative writing, personal experience, and lived experience as an inhabitant of a body read as female and Black. I am also cognizant that a series of troubling displacements must occur for me to frame my preoccupations as "desire," and to describe them through the implicitly objectifying actions of "touch" and "hold." As such, this research is also haunted by the violent histories embedded in the writing context within which I have chosen to articulate it—academic scholarship has long been a colonial vehicle and thus integral to the objectification of female blackness.

I am haunted by the question of what it means to think about female blackness in an academic space particularly as I contemplate Lorde's renown and astute warning of the master's tools' inability to dismantle the master's house.[5] But it is here, within this academic context and the larger historical legacies that shape it, that I am attempting to fashion words to examine silence as a literary tool for Black women writers and by extension Black women who are always on stage in our daily lives. Why academia, as opposed to other mediums whose legacies include long-standing traditions of inhabitants of female Black bodies determining the parameters of our own engagement? My answers are porous, but the most resounding one is that I am drawn to be in conversation with historical and contemporary scholarship created by Black people and specifically Black women. Through its content and context, this body of academic literature positions female Black scholarship as a mode of survival, healing, and mobility in which institutionalized cultures of domination can be disrupted and new articulations of the world imagined. In this regard, it is not the vestiges of Sigmund Freud's theories of desire that motivate this research but a knowing—more akin to Lorde's imagining of a biomythography that can spell one's name anew—that beckons me (1982). The gesture I seek is not to "touch" or "hold" outside of myself but to understand why people in bodies read as female and Black choose dynamic private inner communication and silent public expression (as evidenced, for example, in *At the Full and Change of the Moon*). To this end, I am intrigued by the implications of Adam Jaworski's observation that, "[a]s far as the artistic tradition of the West is concerned, silence is not commonly regarded as a positive means of communication and/or expression" (Jaworski 141).

What might it mean to read Brand's use of public silence in Eula, Maya, and Marie Ursule's lives as acts of resistance (Sandoval 161) that "destabilize the visible" (Elam Jr. 302–3)? To be clear, I am not interested in positing that Brand reclaims silence, whereby what was once perceived as negative is fashioned as positive. Instead, I am interested in what Brand communicates to her readers through her choice to share not only the mostly silent public speech of three of her Black female characters but also their revealing private speech. In "Voice Under Domination: The Arts of Political Disguise," James C. Scott writes "[i]f subordinate groups have typically won a reputation for subtlety—a subtlety their superiors often regard as cunning and deception—this is surely because their vulnerability has rarely permitted them the luxury of direct confrontation" (Scott 136). Thus, my contention is that even though all readers have access to Eula, Maya, and Marie Ursule's public acts and private meditations, attentive readers familiar with the nuances of female blackness will also be able to gain insight through the comparison between what the characters think internally and deem safe and/or worthwhile to say publicly. Jaworski notes that, "communicating in silence may require from the participants more filling in, more completion, and higher participation than communicating in speech ... silence is a medium of communication whose processing requires more cognitive effort than speech" (Jaworski 141). So, who are the attentive readers capable of filling in these spaces in the work of Black women writers?

Henderson theorizes that a central characteristic of Black women's work is heteroglossia and subsequently asks, "Might I suggest that if black women writers speak in tongues, then it is we black feminist critics who are charged with the hermeneutical task of interpreting tongues?" (Henderson 37). According to Henderson, a Black feminist reading of creative work is necessary, one that includes a reader who is not only cognizant of the ways female blackness has been and continues to be silenced but also attentive to how this may materialize in the creative writing of inhabitants of bodies read as female and Black. A Black feminist reading can consider that Black women's literature has been theorized as emerging out of silence, specifically "the inability to express a position in the language of the 'master' as well as the textual construction of woman as silent" (Davies and Fido 1). A Black feminist reading is aided by an understanding of the: interplay of knowledge, wisdom, and experience that Collins asserts is integral to Black feminist epistemologies (1990, 208); choice of silence as a literary device; and ability to interpret the subtle shifts in material conditions that help determine whether silence is advantageous. As such, an attentive, experienced, and thoughtful reader is necessary to carefully contemplate the use and effectiveness of silence.

In Leslie Sanders and Rinaldo Walcott's "At the Full and Change of CanLit: An Interview with Dionne Brand," Brand describes how she approaches a novel, "I begin from the small assumption that it is possible to leap, and that I am curious. The novel doesn't only have to come to me, I need to go to it too. I have to go to the text and I have to say, I'm going to learn some things here" (Sanders and Walcott). There is a way in which the ability to "leap" into other people's realities is a mode of survival and mobility for inhabitants of bodies read as female and Black in Canada. It is a skill that must be learned early and that largely influences one's ability to gain social acceptance in Black and non-Black communities. For inhabitants of bodies read as female and Black in Canada, the ability to "leap" is closely related to one's ability to survive and thrive. My contention is that those in bodies like mine must learn to "leap" because of the same social conditions that create the expectation that Muñoz describes as the "burden of liveness" (Muñoz 187) and that in a Canadian context I call *perpetual performance.*

In *At the Full and Change of the Moon*, Brand takes up the complex implications of the gaze and specifically the difficult experience of being looked at and looking when one inhabits a body read as female and Black in Canada. Eula writes to her dead mother from her home in Toronto, "I am so sick, Mama, so sick from seeing. I wish that I could get my eyesight back where this is only human, what we leave, what we are. I hate this sight of everything" (Brand 240). As in Frantz Fanon and Patricia J. Williams's accounts of the violent experience of being looked at and looking,[6] Eula experiences sight as sickening. Eula implies that the act of looking in Toronto, Canada, in the late-twentieth century involves distortion, if not a complete loss of sight—she wants her "eyesight back" (Brand 240). But the sight that Eula longs to retrieve is one where "there is only human" (Brand 240). As discussed in Chapter 2, "Translucency," seeing "human" is the praxis of translucency that my father, Gerald Belvett, taught me as I stared at my reflection in the mirror: "See a human being first," he said. Eula's lament is a reminder of the challenge of seeing "a human being first" in Canada when one inhabits a body read as female and Black that colonialism and its attendant administrations, institutions, and infrastructures work tirelessly to dehumanize.

Speaking about her writing process, Brand states, "you've got to start really, really tiny. I'm not starting from theme and I'm not starting from some sort of ethnographic drawing. I'm not trying to write a sociological treatise. I'm not starting from there at all" (Sanders and Walcott). I read Brand's articulation of the "really, really tiny" as a powerful assertion that places nuance as the departure point for explorations of the lives of Black people. Through her insistence on imagining the minutiae, Brand subverts hegemonic tropes of blackness that pervade dominant discourse and thrust readers into some of the complex subtleties of Black life. Her emphasis on the "really, really tiny" also signals a feminist writing strategy, one that foregrounds the specific details of life to counteract the ways in which dominant discourses collapse, contain, and omit female realities.

The epigraph that precedes the first chapter of *At the Full and Change of the Moon* is a genealogical chart that begins with the death of Marie Ursule in 1824 and ends with the birth of Eula's daughter Bola in 1982. While Kamena's name appears on the genealogical chart to the right of the line that connects Marie Ursule and Bola, there are no lines that connect Kamena to Marie

Ursule or Bola. In fact, he is the only character who appears on the chart but who has no lines that connect him to the family tree. Furthermore, instead of having a year of birth or death below his name like the other characters, below Kamena's name it reads, "Marooned to his last direction, 1824" though a close reading of the novel reveals that he lived beyond then. Are there gendered readings of Kamena's maroonage on the family tree vis à vis Marie Ursule's explicit genealogical link? In contemporary discourse, it evokes theories of the gendered divisions of labour in Black parenting and it underscores Black nationalisms' essentialist narrative of "Black woman and child" as serving a patriarchal model of Black families. As Judith Butler observes, "just as a script may be enacted in various ways, and just as the play requires both text and interpretation, so the gendered body acts its part in a culturally restricted corporeal space and enacts interpretations within the confines of already existing directives" (Butler 277). However, Kamena subverts the "existing directives" and thus his gendered performance (Butler 277). Kamena longed for freedom, one that he found at Terre Bouillante and one that he left to fulfill a promise to Marie Ursule to return for Bola and lead her out of slavery. In this regard, it is not only blood that Brand privileges as the structure upon which her family tree is based but also loyalty.

A reader of silence might ask, what does Brand communicate through her insistence that Kamena's place in the family lineage be simultaneously visible and ambiguous? Through this silent juxtaposition played out on the genealogical chart, Brand disturbs the structure and function of the family tree—a tree which, by virtue of the legacies of the transatlantic slave trade, is frustratingly impossible for many Black people in North America and the Caribbean to draw. Instead, Brand inscribes Kamena into the historical narrative that the family tree embodies, without adhering to the rules of cartography that define its mapping. Having established this in the epigraph, she unsettles the rules of the family tree further through the character of Bola who has thirteen children with men of varied ethnicities. She names none of the children in commonly practiced ways, but instead names all of them as memories: the one unrecalled, the one who stole her footsteps, the one who loved gold things, the one she washed out with lime, and so on. Some children she keeps, some she gives away, and eventually they are all scattered throughout the diaspora.

As I lay awake early one morning, a heat-filled rage moved through my pregnant body. I was contemplating my pending participation in the Canadian patriarchal tradition of procreation that gives children their fathers' last names. Although I and countless other people with uteruses had experienced the food aversions, nausea, backaches, insomnia, and other symptoms common in pregnancy, the dominant culture in Canada dictates that our last names be invisible as we birth the next generation. My fury was palpable, though the violence of this patriarchal erasure was not a revelation. After years of contemplation, I had finally legally changed my last name in 2005 from my father's surname (Belvett) to my then-middle names (Keleta and Mae) which are the first names of my paternal grandmother and mother. I did this so that my name would embody the balance that I sought. No, this issue was not new to me. Quite the contrary, my husband and I had in-depth discussions about this for years prior to our agreement to attempt conception. And prior to the infuriating moments of that dark morning, I had been comfortable with our decision to name our child with a non-familial first name, a middle name from my family and his last name. But as the sun rose that morning, it felt like a remarkably and painfully insufficient solution. Awash with feminist energy, I ached from the shortcomings of our solution. Had some latent desire to per-form motherhood compromised my ability to do the ever-hard work of more thoughtful debate and imagination?

Brand's focus on the "really, really tiny" (Sanders and Walcott) in the lives of her Black characters is articulated by the absence of two lines that would link Kamena to Marie Ursule and Bola. What this absence or silence can be read to make possible, then, is a subtle and powerful suggestion of how inhabitants of bodies read as Black in Canada might conceptualize anew the framework of the family tree. It is a symbol that persists for many as a site of trauma, emphasizing an unknown history that cannot be charted with the certainty of lines and that does not account for our chosen family—the people with whom we share no genealogical ties but agree to choose as kin. "Our inheritance in the Diaspora is to live in this inexplicable space," Brand says, "That space is the measure of our ancestors' step through the door toward the ship. One is caught in the few feet in between" (Brand 2002, 20). The material repercussions of the millions of people around the world who comprise the African Diaspora being "caught" in a tiny psychic space are far reaching.[7]

# Free

*Music and lyrics by* Naila Keleta-Mae,
Neil Benskin, JahSun Drums, Elijah
Mansevani and Joey Shanahan

Too man - y live in a ten - e - ment Fac - ing prob - lems that just won't re - lent Too man - y failed by the gov - ern - ment Nuff pol - i -

- ti - cians need to re - pent They give ex - cus - es in each in - stant And tell

# 5

## A LETTER

**AS MY PREGNANCY DREW TO A CLOSE,** I began to imagine myself as a mother and I was struck by the wave of political conservatism that engulfed me. I was particularly taken aback by the ways in which I had already begun to perform Black Mother, a stock character problematized by P.H. Collins in "The Meaning of Motherhood in Black Culture and Black Mother/ Daughter Relationships:"

> For those women who either aspire to the cult of true womanhood without the resources to support such a lifestyle or who believe stereotypical analyses of themselves as dominating matriarchs, motherhood can be an oppressive institution. But the experience of motherhood can provide Black women with a base of self-actualization, status in the Black community, and a reason for social activism. These alleged contradictions can exist side by side in African-American communities, families, and even within individual women. (4)

The incongruities Collins identifies were clearly at play in my own psyche. I had already begun to contemplate how I would assert the primacy of my role as Black Mother within my female-dominated immediate and extended family. I had already begun to shape the narrative of the challenges of the first and second trimesters in ways that recounted my experiences but signaled that I possess the strength that is so often associated with female blackness. The feminist Black politics that have underpinned much of my life and work were alarmingly unsettled by an influx of conservative politics. On more than one occasion, I embarked on impassioned soliloquies about why people who want to have children should be married and implied that any other parenting arrangement was insufficient and perhaps morally bankrupt. I stopped short of making the appalling suggestion that only heterosexual couples should be allowed to marry or have children because, I guess somewhere in my psyche, it had occurred to me that such declarations would be blatantly against my own interest—as a bisexual woman I would fail my own litmus test for motherhood and marriage. Indeed, this is not the first time that I have caught myself during a performance that belies my understanding of my politics and reveals instead some of the ways that I perform oppressive notions of personhood. As I sift through my memories, I see a long history of using *this is who I perform* on private and public stage spaces that have comprised daily life since I became cognizant of how my gender and skin colour are read in Canada. And in the moments when *this is who I perform* contradicts with my understanding of myself—the analysis of material conditions, coupled with critical self-reflexivity, provides insights into how deeply ingrained oppressive ideas can be.

As I sit up resoundingly awake in the middle of the night, unable to successfully beckon sleep to relieve me from the drudgery of replaying the series of poor choices I made yesterday, I have concluded that I still have much to learn about how to use *this is who I perform* on the stages that comprise my private and public life. Sometimes, while playing whichever iteration of female blackness *perpetual performance* requires, I find myself furious inside and often when I am furious, I have no idea that I am.

Instead, my fury registers inside me as a gentle nudge, subtle, quiet, and easy to miss until night falls and retrospectives seep in in place of sleep. It is in moments like these that I suffocate in the *perpetual performance* demanded of female blackness in Canada and ache for escape. It is in moments like these that space grows thick and heavy as it flattens hope with despair. It would be easier if these moments only arose after interactions with ideological whiteness. They most often do, but sometimes those moments arise on occasions of performances of female blackness as pre-scribed by other inhabitants of bodies read as female and Black. This is a sentiment that Audre Lorde painfully strips bare in "Eye to Eye: Black Women, Hatred, and Anger":

> Why do Black women reserve a particular voice of fury and disappointment for each other? Who is it we must destroy when we attack each other with that tone of predetermined and correct annihilation? We reduce one another to our own lowest common denominator, and then we proceed to try and obliterate what we most desire to love and touch, the problematic self, unclaimed but fiercely guarded from the other. (159)

Up in the middle of the night again sculpting arguments, rehearsing words. I have learned so much about performing acceptable, respectable, female blackness that confrontations and disagreements cause me stress. I worry I will be unable to find words in the moment to defend and attack. I worry that I will be so disconnected from my actual feelings that I will miss opportunities to respond in the moment with biting wit. My guard is often down. My skin often too thin. I have long envied those able to stand up for themselves in the moment—to be hard when hardness is required. I stew, plan, and practice before confrontations that never unfold as I imagined. I am thinking about the various communities that I am part of and about how we sometimes cling to one another because the rest of the world feels too harsh and judgmental to bear, and so we seek safety and refuge in our commonalities. But I have been in enough communities through enough difficult times to know that they too can be harsh, judgmental, and eerily suffocating because often there is less room for critique and fewer words with which to name the pain we inflict upon one another. I wrote about this in my poem "nine womyn:"

don't go down in those narrow nasty gutters with them
filthy razors be they claws, swaggering
seven womyn of colour cocks, circling

don't go down in the bowels of degradation with them
scheming squealing spinning soul from flesh
now you bloodied bruised discombobulated
and calling them sisters?
fool

of colour don't make them blood
and gender don't mean they care about you

they be marrow-sucking
solidarity-spewing
trifling
bamboozlers
seven of colour womyn
flavoured tangy acrid sour
underbelly masks moulded core in search of fire

cure:


one blossoming gardenia to reignite olfactory
five tablespoons of cod liver oil to cleanse
a heap of sassafras for nurture
repeat in sleep: "no safety there"
and


don't calculate vengeance.
ain't nothing worthwhile nor worthy in it.
just hold on to proper folks:
ones who forgive you wordless
rock you gentle
scoop you up off ceramic
brush foundation on your jaw line
whisper your name when you forget your own damn self
look through you and love sense into you.


hold on to them.
(52–54)


The first time I performed an early version of "nine womyn"
was at the Toronto Women's Bookstore in front of an audience of
mostly minoritized women and men. I was terrified. I had also
learned from years of writing and performing poetry that my
feelings of terror signaled that I had come up against something
that expressed what I was feeling but pushed up hard against what
I thought I could say. For me as an artist that means that I must
speak it aloud in public because, as Lorde reminds us in her poem
"A Litany for Survival," our lives are under threat regardless of
what we do so we might as well be vocal (Lorde 256). At the end

of the performance of my poem, a Black woman in the audience yelled out with laughter in her voice, "You suck Naila." My poem put language to my fears, unsettled ideas I had and called for action that disrupted my notions of feminist solidarity. I wonder if my poem had done similar things to that audience member and others.

For inhabitants of female Black bodies, our daily lives include seeing our female blackness reflected to us in mirrors, windows, and the eyes of adult and children in skin racialized like ours and skin that is not. Surrounded by these refracted images, we are set with the task of resistance and imagination. My contention throughout this book has been that inhabitants of bodies read as female and Black in Canada imagine *this is who I perform* as a response to dominant discourses and cultures that impose anti-blackness and misogyny on female blackness. Indeed, it is challenging to be compelled to perform by those of other genders and/or skin colours; however, it is particularly difficult when the expectation of performance comes from someone who is also female and Black.

*My babies,*

*I remember when they laid each of you, newly born onto my chest—one in 2010 and one in 2013. I love you.*

*I am writing you this letter in keeping with our family's letter writing tradition. My mother, father, and maternal grandmother wrote me letters throughout my life so, here I am, writing you. Sometimes I feel overwhelmed by all that I want to tell you and all that I want to protect you from. Sometimes I am seized by fear. You have brown skin in a country where brown skin is seen as inferior. I love you, and what is perhaps most difficult is knowing that the profound love I have for you cannot protect you from what it means to look like us in this country.*

My parents moved to Winnipeg, Canada, from Saint Catherine, Jamaica, in the 1960s. Though they were not descendants of the Black Canadians who have lived here since the seventeenth century, they were privy to some of the legacies of racism that marred Canada long before Confederation. Apartments advertised as vacant immediately became occupied once superintendents answered doorbells and saw my brown-skinned parents standing on their doorsteps. However, it was also the dawn of the Pierre Elliott Trudeau era that heralded the promise of a new Canada. My parents decided to stay, later have two children, enroll us in French Immersion and be community organizers while pursuing their respective careers. They were adamant that my sister and I had no Jamaican "home" to go back to. Their message was clear— Canada was our home; we were not to allow others to treat us otherwise and we had to be what my mother called "good citizens of the world."

Most weekday mornings my mother left for work before I left for school. Her commute by public transit to the heart of the financial district downtown where she worked from the suburbs where we lived was about ninety minutes one way. Many mornings I would sit on my parents' bed and watch her race through her morning routine. My memories are vivid: Mom standing in her closet deciding which blouse to wear with which of her Alfred Sung or Jones New York suits, then pairing the sophisticated ensemble with pantyhose, earrings, necklace, pumps, purse and a spritz of perfume. From the vantage point of my parents' bed, I also had a great view of the bathroom where my mom would lean over the counter as she curled her hair and applied her make-up. I loved watching her daily ritual of transformation and inhaling the scents of coffee, perfume and hair oil burning on a hot curling iron. My father must have been in the room many of those mornings too, though my memories of his getting dressed are vague. Sometimes *he would ask me to help him choose a tie and sometimes, after he shaved, he would touch a bit of cologne to my neck as I stood beside him by his chest of drawers. I learned much about performance those mornings as I bounced on their bed and raced in and out of their bathroom while they prepared to face the world outside of our home. I learned much about how to compose one's image to facilitate one's relationship with the world and much about the necessity of this exercise. I later learned much more about the tremendous power that lies in the rituals of corporal composition of femaleness and blackness that I witnessed, participated in, and experimented with as a child, teenager and now adult.*

*I started learning French when I was four years old. I am teaching you French because I want you to learn it earlier and better than I did. My parents rarely spoke Jamaican to us. They wanted us to fit in. I learned Jamaican as an adult because I needed more ways to understand the world and my place in it than English and French could afford me. That is why sometimes I speak to you in Jamaican. I want you to have many languages at your disposal, many ways to communicate the complexities of your thoughts and realities. As for a home to go back to? Well, go where you need to go. Build what you need to build. Make your home inside of you. Know that your ancestors move with you and always prepare a home for you. It also never hurts to carry meaningful bits with you, a couple of hymns, a poem or two and a few good recipes.*

*The blessing ceremony we held for each of you at our home when you were babies was created in consultation with the minister who officiated it. There was water, a candle, and no religious vows. Instead, in front of family and friends, your father and I promised to support you on your spiritual journey, encourage you to discover and realize the objectives of your life, and guide you towards a life of honor and integrity. The following excerpt of "Children," by Khalil Gibran, was read by my sister, Gail:*

Your children are not your children. They are the sons and
daughters of Life's longing for itself. They come through you
but not from you, And though they are with you, yet they
belong not to you. You may give them your love but not your
thoughts, For they have their own thoughts. You may house
their bodies but not their souls, For their souls dwell in the
house of tomorrow, which you cannot visit, not even in
your dreams. You may strive to be like them, but seek not to
make them like you. For life goes not backward nor tarries
with yesterday

You are the bows from which your children as living arrows
are sent forth. (17)

*You do not belong to me. You are each your own person. I share
my experiences with you and my strategies not only for survival
but also for success, all the while knowing that the contexts that
shape your life are different than the ones that shape my own. The
pressures that you feel, joy you experience, and strategies you develop are appropriate for you. I am learning from you. I want you
to imagine, discover, fail, recover, and realize your own dreams.
Thank you for choosing me to be your mother. I will do my very best.*

*Je vous aime,*
*Maman.*

### Chapter 1: Female and Black

1  I wrote this passage when I was pregnant in 2009–10. These were the statistics based on the then most recent census conducted in 2006.

2  See Andrea A. Davis (2004) for a thoughtful analysis of nation, blackness, and womanhood. Davis 2022 was published as I was preparing the final manuscript and thus, unfortunately, it is not taken up in this book.

3  "Free" was originally performed by Neil Benskin, JahSun Drums, Elijah Mansevani, Joey Shanahan, and Naila Keleta-Mae. The sheet music was transcribed by Cameron Slipp.

4  For more, see Cooper, Afua. 2006. *The Hanging of Angélique: The Untold Story of Canadian Slavery and the Burning of Old Montreal*, HarperCollins.

5  See Moraga and Anzaldúa; Lorde (1984a); Madison; Ebron and Tsing; Dicker/sun; Philip for more.

6  406A also appears in my play *stuck* but as the room number in a psychiatric ward of a hospital.

### Chapter 2: Translucency

1  See Dussel "From the Invention to the Discovery of the New World," 34 for a productive example of how colonial processes necessitate the "covering over" of "native" bodies.

2  See Marianna Torgovnick's "Defining the Primitive/Reimagining Modernity" for descriptions of relationships between the word "primitive" and the construction of Modernity.

3  See Bruce D. Dickson Jr.'s *The "John and Old Master" Stories and the World of Slavery: A Study in Folktales and History* for a discussion of the long tradition in African American culture and history of manipulating performance.

4  See Suzan-Lori Parks's play *Venus* for her imaginative portrayal of
the interior life of Sarah Baartman, one that moves her experience
from one that is solely about survival to one that is speckled with
moments of agency.

5  In *Black Feminist Thought: Knowledge, Consciousness, and the
Politics of Empowerment*, Patricia Hill Collins remarks,

> An alternative epistemology challenges all certified
> knowledge and opens up the question of whether what
> has been taken to be true can stand the test of alternative
> ways of validating truth. The existence of a self-defined
> Black women's standpoint using an Afrocentric feminist
> epistemology calls into question the content of what
> currently passes as truth and simultaneously challenges
> the process of arriving at truth. (219)

6  Lyricist unknown. The arrangement for this hymn is attributed
to Phil Lindsley.

7  The 1970s and early 1980s saw a flurry of writing by women of colour
that challenged existing feminist discourse on multiple planes namely
for its lack of consideration of race, class, and sexual orientation.
*The Bridge Called My Back: Writings by Radical Women of Color*,
edited by Cherríe Moraga and Gloria Anzaldúa and *Ain't I A Woman:
Black Women and Feminism* by bell hooks are landmark examples.

8  As expressed by bell hooks in "naked without a shame: a counter-
hegemonic body politic."

9  See Franz Kafka's "In the Penal Colony."

10 See Jacques Lacan's "The mirror stage as formative of the function
of the I as revealed in psychoanalytic experience."

11 See Larry Neale's "The Black Arts Movement."

12 See Shireen Hassim's *Women's Organizations and Democracy in
South Africa*.

## Chapter 3: Made Public

1  Edited by Karen Richardson and Steven Green.

2  Edited by Valerie Mason-John and Kevan Anthony Cameron.

3  I changed my last name to Keleta-Mae from Belvett in 2005 so this
   entry appears under the name Belvett in the Works Cited section.
4  This analysis draws from Naila Keleta-Mae's "angry black bitch
   sister nigga: Sexualized Performances for the Nations."
5  José Esteban Muñoz writes:

> Think, for a moment, of the queer revolutionary
> from the Antilles, perhaps a young woman who has
> already been burned in Fanon's text by his writing
> on the colonized woman. What process can keep an
> identification with Fanon, his politics, his work possible
> for this woman? In such a case, a disidentification with
> Fanon might be one of the only ways in which she is
> capable of reformatting the powerful theorist for her
> own project, one that might be as queer and feminist
> as it is anticolonial. Disidentification offers a Fanon,
> for that queer and lesbian reader, who would not be
> sanitized; instead, his homophobia and misogyny would
> be interrogated while his anticolonial discourse was
> engaged as a *still* valuable yet mediated identification. (9)

6  "[w]hile at the beginning the native intellectual used to produce
   his work to be read exclusively by the oppressor, whether with the
   intention of charming him or of denouncing him through ethnic
   or subjectivist means, now the native writer progressively takes on
   the habit of addressing his own people" ("National" 120).
7  In *Inna di Dancehall: Popular Culture and the Politics of Identity
   in Jamaica*, Donna P. Hope observes that,

> [w]here sexuality is concerned, the Madonna/whore
> syndrome is transformed by these additional factors to
> produce the race- and class-influenced "ghetto slam"
> (ghetto sex) ideology. A man can get a ghetto slam
> from a *trang* (strong) Black woman from the lower or
> working class or from the inner city—a Black lower-
> working-class phenomenon. This woman is believed

> to have the physical make-up that makes her suitable
> for engagement in overtly physical displays of sexual
> activity—large breast, large posterior, big frame. (40–41)

8   See bell hooks, *Ain't I A Woman: Black Women and Feminism* and
Michele Wallace, "The Myth of the Superwoman."

9   "suicide. Suicide. Suicide. Hovers on the breath, in the realms of
thought of all the so-called strong/black/womyn/warriors i know"
(Belvett).

10  The deleted text from "star:"

> shit.
> now what the fuck am i supposed to do with that?
> why ya got to go and kill the dream? i'm not trying
> to hear that folks are jumping through similar hoops
> a continent away. damn. that's supposed to be the
> motherland. that sweet sweet place called home. that
> place where i and millions of other lost children of the
> african diaspora can go to just 'chill out' not have our
> brains spill out on pavement/cement tenements the
> same way it is here.
> (i need a space where i can grow out of harm way/i'm
> Black u see.)
>
> ---
>
> fuck.
> struggling i am. enticed by the perceived beauty and the
> lure of that sweet sweet Black suburban bourgeoisie. and
> what's the alternative? actually live the politics i spew
> in 'conscious' social circles? damn all that "revolution
> of self" talk makes me nauseous. i'm trying to be like
> bob—well at least like buju, so i can talk about the
> struggles of poverty when i'm straight rolling. why can't
> i just be profiling? u know, make nuff loot and have nuff
> access to comfort before i get too stressed out about
> global details.

...

i'm saying. i'll wear my army fatigues to keep it real,
some old school darkers, phat boots and a fine leather
jacket by day. (night time's private.)
lawd a mercy.
wha gwan?
ah dat mi wan fi know.

...

and somewhere inside i know there isn't enough
stuff in the world to make me feel better, but i'll
probably die before i stop trying to buy my way out of
emptiness. how much do i have to unlearn and how
much work do i really have to put in? ah hell. sick just
thinking about it.

...

fly body, fairly steady mentally

...

well i'm that nigga who's tired of trying to fit.

...

all this to say. i've got so much floating in my head
and in the receses of my psyche that i can't even begin
to take on anything more than my own tears/fears.
selfish. i know. i am. trying to keep it 'real' with me
first. i know. i am. interior walls of defense are thick
and reinforced with steel. my soul.

...

u know this world has been ruled by male misogynist
energy for so fucking long

...

send blessings. we need them.

from the cold north,
naila

11 See Katherine McKittrick's "Nothing's Shocking: Black Canada" for a discussion on how and to what end "surprise" and "wonder" are routinely associated with blackness in Canada.

12 "lawd a mercy. / wha gwan? / ah dat mi wan fi know"

13 "i'm trying to be like bob [marley]—well at least like buju [banton], so i can talk about the struggles of poverty when i'm straight rolling."

14 "why ya got to go and kill the [Martin Luther King Jr. and Langston Hughes] dream? / ... / enticed by the perceived beauty and the lure of that sweet sweet Black suburban bourgeoisie"

15 "fairly steady mentally / ... / i've got so much floating in my head and in the recesses of my psyche that i can't even begin to take on anything more than my own tears/fears."

16 This analysis draws from Naila Keleta-Mae's "Body and Text."

17 See chapter 1 of Ruth Behar's *The Vulnerable Observer: Anthropology That Breaks Your Heart*, for a discussion on the challenges of locating oneself within one's own text.

18 Italics sung by actor.

19 This excerpt is based on my personal experience of presenting "On Glass Ceilings, Feminism and Safety" as the Distinguished Guest Speaker at the University of Waterloo International Women's Day Dinner in 2017. Shortly thereafter, I received an email with "Confidential" in the subject line from someone who attended the dinner, identified as a middle-aged white woman and argued that my speech should have given more consideration to people in her demographic.

## Chapter 4: Silence

1 In "The Black Performer and the Performance of Blackness," Harry J. Elam Jr. describes these performances as "The Mask, the device of a differentiated performance of blackness solely for the white gaze, [the mask] helped Blacks to negotiate the dangers of racism and oppression" (294).

2  The following is Lorde's description of poetry as illumination:

> The quality of light by which we scrutinize our lives
> has direct bearing upon the product which we live,
> and upon the changes which we hope to bring about
> through those lives. It is within this light that we form
> those ideas by which we pursue our magic and make it
> realized. This is poetry as illumination (36).

3  The mobilization of the very mode of oppression one seeks to disrupt recalls my discussion in the chapter "Translucency" of Anne McClintock's assertion that "[c]olonialism returns at the moment of its disappearance" (11).

4  She administers but does not take the poison with the others so that she can see the plantation owner's reaction and tell him that she devised the plot.

5  See Lorde's "The Master's Tools Will Never Dismantle the Master's House."

6  See Chapter 2, "Translucency."

7  For example, with regards to impacts on students Rinaldo Walcott asserts that, "[i]t is the inability to work through this repressed trauma that leaves Black students continually repeating the condition of being in pain as the basis of identity and community formation" (137).

## WORKS CITED

Abbas, Nuzhat. 1999. "Dionne's Brand of Writing." *Herizons,* vol. 13, no. 3: 18–22. *ProQuest,* search.proquest.com.proxy.lib.uwaterloo.ca/magazines/dionnes-brand-writing/docview/212382076/se-2

Anghie, Antony. 2002. "Colonialism and the Birth of International Institutions: Sovereignty, Economy, and the Mandate System of the League of Nations." *New York University Journal of International Law and Politics,* vol. 34, no. 3: 513–634. ocul-wtl.primo.exlibrisgroup.com/permalink/01OCUL_WTL/3b6rcr/cdi_proquest_miscellaneous_60653453

anitafrika, d'bi.young. 2006. *Blood.claat = Sangre.* Translated by Queen Nzinga and Maxwell Edwards. 1st ed., Playwrights Canada Press.

anthony, trey. 2010. *'Da Kink in My Hair.* 2nd ed., Playwrights Canada Press.

Anzaldúa, Gloria. 1981. "Speaking In Tongues: A Letter to 3rd World Women Writers." *This Bridge Called My Back: Writings by Radical Women of Color,* edited by Cherríe Moraga and Gloria Anzaldúa, 1st ed., Kitchen Table Press, 165–74.

Bakare-Yusuf, Bibi. 1999. "The Economy of Violence: Black Bodies and the Unspeakable Terror." *Feminist Theory and the Body: A Reader,* edited by Janet Price and Margrit Shildrick, Routledge, 311–23.

Bambara, Toni Cade. 1980. *The Salt Eaters.* 1st ed., Random House.

Bannerji, Himani. 2000. *The Dark Side of the Nation: Essays on Multiculturalism, Nationalism and Gender.* Canadian Scholars' Press.

Behar, Ruth. 1996. *The Vulnerable Observer: Anthropology That Breaks Your Heart.* Beacon Press, 1–33.

Belvett, Naila. 2001. "stuck." personal collection of Naila Keleta-Mae, Toronto, 1–42.

———. 2002. "star" excerpt from "Bantu Serenade." *Chimurenga: Biko In Parliament, v*ol. 3, edited by Ntone Edjabe, Pan African Market Press, Cape Town, 63.

Bennett, Susan. 1990. *Theatre Audiences: A Theory of Production and Reception.* Routledge.

Benz, Spragga. "Jack It Up." *Apple Music.* music.apple.com/ca/album/jack-it-up/309413216?i=309413283

Biemann, Ursula. 2002. "Performing the Border: On Gender, Transnational Bodies, and Technology." *Globilization on the Line: Culture, Capital, and Citizenship at U.S. Borders.* Edited by Claudia Sadowski-Smith, Palgrave, 99–118.

bissett, bill and Adeena Karasick. 2007. "Shards of Light." *Canadian Theatre Review,* no. 130: 15–20.

Brand, Dionne. 1999. *At the Full and Change of the Moon.* Alfred A. Knopf Canada.

———. 2002. *A Map to the Door of No Return: Notes to Belonging.* Vintage Canada.

Breon, Robin. 2005. "The Growth and Development of Black Theatre in Canada: A Starting Point." *African-Canadian Theatre. Critical Perspectives on Canadian Theatre in English,* vol. 2, edited by Maureen Moynagh, Playwrights Canada Press, 1–10.

Broox, Klyde. 2007. "Gestures of the Dancing Voice: Reloading the Can(n)on Under the Influence of Dub." *Canadian Theatre Review,* no. 130: 72–82.

Brown, William. 1858. *The Escape; Or, A Leap for Freedom: A Drama in Five Acts.* Sabin Americana 1500–1926, R.F. Wallcut.

Browne, Simone. 2015. *Dark Matters: On the Surveillance of Blackness.* Duke University Press.

Butler, Judith. 1990. "Performative Acts and Gender Constitution." *Performing Feminisms: Feminist Critical Theory and Theatre,* edited by Sue-Ellen Case, The John Hopkins Press, 270–82.

Christian, Barbara. 1988. "The Race for Theory." *Feminist Studies,* vol.14, no.1 (Spring): 67–79.

Codrington, Lisa. 2006. *Cast Iron.* 1st ed., Playwrights Canada Press.

Collins, Patricia Hill. 1987. "The Meaning of Motherhood in Black Culture and Black Mother/Daughter Relationships." *Sage:: A Scholarly Journal on Black Woman*, vol. 4, no. 2, 3–10.

———. 1990. *Black Feminist Thought: Knowledge, Consciousness, and the Politics of Empowerment.* Unwin Hyman.

———. 2004. *Black Sexual Politics: African Americans, Gender, and the New Racism.* Routledge.

———. 2006. *From Black Power to Hip Hop: Racism, Nationalism, and Feminism.* Temple University Press.

Combahee River Collective. 1984. "A Black Feminist Statement." *The Bridge Called My Back: Writings by Radical Women of Color,* edited by Cherríe Moraga and Gloria Anzaldúa, Kitchen Table Press, 210–18.

Cowan, T.L., editor. 2007. *Spoken Word Performance,* special issue of *Canadian Theatre Review,* no. 130.

Crenshaw, Kimberlé Williams. 1994. "Demarginalizing the Intersection of Race and Sex: A Black Feminist Critique of Antidiscrimination Doctrine, Feminist Theory, and Antiracist Politics." *Living with Contradictions: Controversies in Feminist Social Ethics,* edited by Alison M. Jaggar, Westview Press, 39–52.

Davies, Carole Boyce and Elaine Savory Fido. 1990. "Women and Literature in the Caribbean: An Overview." *Out of the Kumbla: Caribbean Women and Literature,* Africa World Press, 1–24.

Davis, Andrea A. 2004. "Diaspora, Citizenship and Gender: Challenging the Myth of the Nation in African Canadian Women's Literature." *Canadian Woman Studies,* vol. 23, no. 2, 64–69.

———. 2005. "Sex and the Nation: Performing Black Female Sexuality in Canadian Theatre." *African-Canadian Theatre: Critical Perspectives on Canadian Theatre in English, v*ol. 2, edited by Maureen Moynagh, Playwrights Canada Press, 107–21.

———. 2022. *Horizon, Sea, Sound: Caribbean and African Women's Cultural Critiques of Nation.* Northwestern University Press.

Davis, Angela Yvonne. 1998. "'Strange Fruit': Music and Social Consciousness." *Blues Legacies and Black Feminism: Gertrude "Ma" Rainey, Bessie Smith, and Billie Holiday,* Random House, 181–97.

Dicker/sun, Glenda. 1996. "Festivities and Jubilations on the Graves of the Dead: Sanctifying sullied space." *Performance and Cultural Politics,* edited by Elin Diamond, Routledge, 108–27.

Dickson Jr., Bruce D. 1974. "The 'John and Old Master' Stories and the World of Slavery: A Study in Folktales and History." *Phylon,* vol. 35, no. 4, 418–29. doi.org/10.2307/274744.

Duncan, Margot. 2004. "Autoethnography: Critical Appreciation of an Emerging Art." *International Journal of Qualitative Methods* vol. 3, no. 4, 28–39. doi.org/10.1177/160940690400300403.

Dussel, Enrique. 1995. "From the Invention to the Discovery of the New World." *The Invention of the Americas: Eclipse of 'the other' and the Myth of Modernity,* translated by Michel D. Barber, Continuum, 27–36.

Dyson, Michael Eric. 1999. "Be Like Mike? Michael Jordan and the Pedagogy of Desire." *Signifyin(g), Sanctifyin' & Slam Dunking: A Reader in African American Expressive Culture,* edited by Gena Dagel Caponi, University of Massachusetts Press, 407–16.

Eagly, Alice H. 2012. "Women as Leaders: Progress Through the Labyrinth." *Social Categories in Everyday Experience*, edited by S Wiley, G. Philogène and T. A. Revenson, APA Books, 64–65.

Ebron, Paulla A. and Anna Lowenhaupt Tsing. 1995. "In Dialogue? Reading Across Minority Discourses." *Women Writing Culture*, edited by Ruth Behar and Deborah A. Gordon, University of California Press, 390–411.

Elam Jr., Harry J. 2001. "The Black Performer and the Performance of Blackness." *African American Performance and Theater History: A Critical Reader,* edited by Harry J. Elam Jr and David Krasner, Oxford University Press, 288–305.

Ellis, C. 1999. "Heartful Autoethnography." *Qualitative Health Research* vol. 9, no. 5, 669–83.

Evans, Ammoye. "Don't Count Me Out." *YouTube Music.* https://music.youtube.com/watch?v=_vjcComCk2g&feature=share

Fanon, Frantz. 1967. "The Fact of Blackness." *Black Skin, White Masks.* Grove Press, 109–40.

———. 2006. "National Culture." *The Post-Colonial Studies Reader,* 2nd ed. Edited by Bill Aschcroft, Gareth Griffiths and Helen Tiffin, Routledge, 119–22.

Filewod, Alan. 2005. "'From Twisted History': Reading Angélique." *African-Canadian Theatre. Critical Perspectives on Canadian Theatre in English,* vol. 2, Playwrights Canada Press, 29–39.

Fleetwood, Nicole. 2011. "Excess Flesh: Black Women Performing Hypervisibility." *Troubling Vision: Performance, Visuality, and Blackness,* University of Chicago Press, 105–46.

Gale, Lorena. 1999. *Angélique.* Playwrights Canada Press.

———. 2001. *Je Me Souviens.* Talonbooks.

Gibran, Khalil. 2009. "Children." *The Prophet.* Floating Press, 17–18.

Gibson, Nigel. 2006. "Fanon, Marx, and the New Reality of the Nation: Black Political Empowerment and the Challenge of a New Humanism in South Africa." *Articulations: A Harold Wolpe Memorial Lecture Collection,* edited by Amanda Alexander. Africa World Press, 113–38.

Gordone, Charles. 1969. *No Place to Be Somebody: A Black Black Comedy in Three Acts.* Bobbs-Merrill.

Hassim, Shireen. 2006. *Women's Organizations and Democracy in South Africa.* University of Wisconsin Press.

Henderson, Mae Gwendolyn. 1989. "Speaking in Tongues: Dialogics, Dialectics, and the Black Woman Writer's Literary Tradition." *Changing our own Words: Essays on Criticism, Theory, and Writing by Black Women,* edited by Cheryl A. Wall, Rutgers University Press, 16–37.

Holt, Grace Sims. 1972. "Stylin' Outta the Black Pulpit." *Signifyin(g), Sanctifyin' and Slam Dunking: A Reader in African American Expressive Culture,* edited by Gena Dagel Caponi, University of Massachusetts Press, 1999, 331–47.

hooks, bell. 1981. *Ain't I A Woman: Black Women and Feminism.* South End Press.

———. 1998. "naked without a shame: a counter-hegemonic body politic." *Talking Visions: Multicultural Feminisms in a Transnational Age,* edited by Ella Shohat, The MIT Press, 65–74.

——. 1992. "The Oppositional Gaze: Black Female Spectatorship." *Black Looks: Race and Representation,* Between the Lines, 115–31.

Hope, Donna P. 2006. *Inna di Dancehall: Popular Culture and the Politics of Identity in Jamaica.* University of the West Indies Press.

Hurston, Zora Neale. 1942. "How It Feels to Be Colored Me." *I Love Myself When I Am Laughing... And Then Again When I Am Looking Mean and Impressive: A Zora Neale Hurston Reader,* edited by Alice Walker, The Feminist Press, 1979, 152–55.

Hussain, Nasser. 2007. "Consuming Language: Embodiment in the Performance Poetry of bpNichol and Steve McCaffery." *Canadian Theatre Review,* no. 130, 21–25.

Jaworski, Adam. 1993. *The Power of Silence: Social and Pragmatic Perspectives.* Sage Publications.

Johnson, Patrick E. 2003. "Sounds of Blackness Down Under: The Café of the Gate of Salvation." *Appropriating Blackness,* Duke University Press, 160–218.

Jones, El. 2014. *Live from the Afrikan Resistance!* Roseway Publishing, an imprint of Fernwood Publishing.

Kafka, Franz. 1948. "In the Penal Colony." *The Penal Colony,* translated by Willa and Edwin Muir, Schocken Books, 191–227.

Keleta-Mae, Naila. 2007. "No Knowledge College." *Canadian Theatre Review,* no. 130, 101–7.

——. 2007. "nine womyn." *Some Poems By People I Like.* Edited by Sandra Alland, sandraslittlebookshop, 52–54.

——. 2009a. "angry black bitch sister nigga: Sexualized Performances for the Nations." *alt.theatre: cultural diversity and the stage.* Teesri Duniya Theatre, vol. 7, no. 1, 20–25.

——. 2009b. "this is my rant." *Apple Music.* https://music.apple.com/us/album/this-is-my-rant/1514732153?i=1514732154

——. 2012. "mother tongue." Personal collection of Naila Keleta-Mae, Toronto.

——. 2015. "An autoethnographic reading of Djanet Sears's The Adventures of a Black Girl in Search of God." *Theatre Research in Canada / Recherches théatrales au Canada,* vol. 36, no. 1, 73–88.

———. 2017. "*on love:* Performance as pedagogy." *Performance Studies in Canada*, edited by Laura Levin and Marlis Schweitzer, McGill-Queen's University Press, 316–39.

———. 2020. "Writing with Sound in *What We Deserve.*" *Canadian Theatre Review*, no. 184, 39–41.

Keleta-Mae, Naila, et al. "Free." *Apple Music.* https://music.apple.com/us/album/fire-woman/1499603335. Sheet music transcribed by Cameron Slipp.

Kinaschuk, Kyle. 2020. "Hearing Zong! Choreosonographies of Silence." *Studies in Canadian Literature/Études en littérature canadienne*, vol. 45, no. 1, 49–73. doi.org/10.7202/1075585ar.

Lacan, Jacques. 1977. "The mirror stage as formative of the function of the I as revealed in psychoanalytic experience." *Écrits: A Selection*, translated by Alan Sheridan, Tavistock, 1–7.

Latifah, Queen featuring Monie Love. "Ladies First." *Apple Music*, https://music.apple.com/ca/album/ladies-first-feat-monie-love -queen-latifah-monie-love/1604628749?i=1604628753.

Lee, Angela. 1995. "ahdri zhina mandiela: Encountering Signposts (Interview)." *Canadian Theatre Review*, no. 83, 5–8.

Lindsley, Phil V.S., arranger. 1923. "Got a Home in That Rock." *National Baptist Jubilee Melodies*, National Baptist Publishing Board, 49.

Lorde, Audre. 1982. *Zami: A New Spelling of My Name.* The Crossing Press.

———. 1984a. *Sister Outsider: Essays and Speeches by Audre Lorde.* The Crossing Press.

———. 1984b. "Eye to Eye: Black Women, Hatred, and Anger." *Sister Outsider: Essays and Speeches by Audre Lorde.* The Crossing Press, 145–75.

———. 1984c. "The Master's Tools Will Never Dismantle the Master's House." *Sister Outsider: Essays and Speeches by Audre Lorde.* The Crossing Press, 110–13.

———. 1998. "Poetry is not a Luxury." *Sister Outsider: Essays and Speeches by Audre Lorde,* 1984, The Crossing Press, 36–39.

———. 2000. "A Litany for Survival." *The Collected Poems of Audre Lorde.* 1st pbk. ed., W.W. Norton, 255–56.

mandiela, ahdri zhina. 1991. *Dark Diaspora—in DUB: a dub theatre piece.* Sister Vision Press.

——. 2012. *Who knew grannie: a dub aria.* Playwrights Canada Press.

Madison, D. Soyini. 1994. "Introduction." *The Woman That I Am: The Literature and Culture of Contemporary Women of Color,* edited by D. Soyini Madison, St. Martin's Griffin, 1–18.

——. 2006. "Staging Fieldwork/Performing Human Rights." *The Sage Handbook of Performance Studies,* edited by D. Soyini Madison and Judith Hamera, Sage Publications, 397–418.

——. 2014. *Black Performance Theory,* edited by Thomas F. DeFrantz and Anita Gonzalez, Duke University Press.

Mason-John, Valerie and Kevan Anthony Cameron, editors. 2013. *The Great Black North: Contemporary African Canadian Poetry.* Frontenac House Poetry.

Maynard, Robyn. 2017. *Policing Black Lives: State Violence in Canada from Slavery to the Present.* Fernwood Press.

McClaurin, Irma. 2001. "Theorizing a Black Feminist Self in Anthropology: Toward an Autoethnographic Approach." *Black Feminist Anthropology: Theory, Politics, Praxis, and Poetics,* edited by Irma McClaurin, Rutgers University Press, 49–76.

McClintock, Anne. 1995. *Imperial Leather: Race, Gender and Sexuality in the Colonial Contest.* Routledge.

McKittrick, Katherine. 2006. "Nothing's Shocking: Black Canada." *Demonic Grounds: Black Women and the Cartographies of Struggle,* University of Minnesota Press, 91–119.

Minh-ha, Trinh T. 1989. "Difference: A Special Third World Women Issue." *Woman, Native Other: Writing Postcoloniality and Feminism,* Indiana University Press, 79–116.

Moraga, Cherríe and Gloria Anzaldúa, editors. 1981. *This Bridge Called My Back: Writings by Radical Women of Color,* Kitchen Table Press, 165–74.

Muñoz, José Esteban. 1999. *Disidentifications: Queers of Color and the Performance of Politics.* University of Minnesota Press.

Natural, Cherry. 2003. *Earth Woman: Selected Poems 1989–2001,* edited by Jahn D. Galuska, Rastazumska Productions.

Ndegeocello, Meshell. 1993. "I'm Diggin You (Like an Old Soul Record)." *Plantation Lullabies,* Maverick Records.

Neal, Larry. Summer 1968. "The Black Arts Movement." *The Drama Review TDR,* vol. 12, no. 4, MIT Press, 29–39.

Parks, Suzan-Lori. 1997. *Venus: A Play.* Theatre Communications Group.

Parris, Amanda. 2019. *Other Side of the Game.* 1st ed., Playwrights Canada Press.

Philip, M. Nourbese. 2008. "Notanda." *Zong!.* Wesleyan University Press, 187–207.

Postcard. Publicity materials from 2001 workshop production of *stuck.*

Reed-Danahay, D. 1997. *Auto/ethnography: Rewriting the Self and the Social.* Berg.

Richardson, Karen and Steven Green, editors. 2004. *T-Dot Griots: An anthology of Toronto's Black Storytellers,* Trafford Publishing.

Rose, Tricia. 1991. "'Fear of a Black Planet': Rap Music and Black Cultural Politics in the 1990s." *The Journal of Negro Education,* vol. 60, no. 3 (Summer): 276–90. doi.org/10.2307/2295482.

Sanders, Leslie and Rinaldo Walcott. 2000. "At the Full and Change of CanLit: An Interview with Dionne Brand." *Canadian Woman Studies,* vol. 20, no. 2, 22+ *Gale Academic OneFile.* https://link.gale.com/apps/doc/A70970941/AONE?u=uniwater&sid=bookmarkONE&xid=5c169a63.

Sandoval, Chela. 2000. "Revolutionary Force: Connecting Desire to Reality." *Methodology of the Oppressed,* University of Minnesota Press, 159–78.

Scott, James C. 1990. "Voice under Domination: The Arts of Political Disguise." *Domination and the Arts of Resistance: Hidden Transcripts,* Yale University Press, 136–82.

Sears, Djanet. 1997. *Harlem Duet.* Scirocco Drama.

———. 2000a. "Introduction." *Testifyin': Contemporary African Canadian Drama Vol. 1,* edited by Djanet Sears, Playwrights Canada Press, i–xiii.

———. 2000b. "The Adventures of a Black Girl in Search of God. *Testifyin': Contemporary African Canadian Drama Vol. 2,* edited by Djanet Sears, Playwrights Canada Press, 491–604.

Sharpe, Christina. 2016. *In the Wake: On Blackness and Being,* Duke University Press.

Siklosi, Kate. 2016. "'The Absolute / of Water': The Submarine Poetic of M. NourbeSe Philip's Zong!" *Canadian Literature,* no. 228, 111–30, 269. *ProQuest,* http://search.proquest.com.proxy.lib.uwaterloo.ca/

scholarly-journals/absolute-water-submarine-poetic-m-nourbese/docview/1882452549/se-2.

Smallwood, Richard. "The Center of My Joy." *YouTube Music*. https://music.youtube.com/watch?v=IozJDb0EwoQ&feature=share.

Spillers, Hortense. 1987. "Mama's Baby, Papa's Maybe: An American Grammar Book". *Diacritics*, vol. 17, no. 2, 65–81. doi.org/10.2307/464747.

Stanton, Victoria, and Vincent Tinguely, editors. 2001. *Impure: Reinventing the Word: The Theory, Practice, and Oral History of 'Spoken Word' in Montreal*. conundrum press.

Statistics Canada. 2022. "The Canadian Census: A Rich Portrait of the Country's Religious and Ethnocultural Diversity." 1–25.

——. 2008. Canada's Ethnocultural Mosaic, 2006 Census: Highlights. *Statistics Canada Catalogue*, no. 97–562.

Stephens, Tanya. "You nuh ready fi dis yet." *Youtube*. https://youtu.be/NdetcZXF9gs

"Text of Clinton's 2008 Concession Speech," *The Guardian* (U.K.), June 7, 2008.

Torgovnick, Marianna. 1990. "Defining the Primitive/Reimagining Modernity." *Gone Primitive: Savage Intellects, Modern Lives*, University of Chicago Press, 3–41.

Van Fossen, Rachael. 13 December 2007. Personal interview.

Walcott, Rinaldo. 2000. "Pedagogy and Trauma: The Middle Passage, Slavery, and the Problem of Creolization." *Between Hope and Despair: Pedagogy and the Remembrance of Historical Trauma*, edited by Roger J. Simon, Sharon Rosenberg and Claudia Eppert, Rowman & Littlefield Publishers, 135–51.

Wallace, Michele. 1979. "The Myth of the Superwoman." *Black Macho and the Myth of the Superwoman,* Verso, 1990, pp. 87–177.

Williams, Patricia J. 1997. "On Being the Object of Property." *Writing on the Body: Female Embodiment and Feminist Theory,* edited by K. Conboy, et al., Columbia Press, 155–75.

Willis, Deborah. 2010. *Black Venus 2010: They Called Her "Hottentot."* Temple University Press.

Wynter, Sylvia. 1990. "Beyond Miranda's Meanings: Un/silencing the 'Demonic Ground' of Caliban's 'Woman.'" *Out of the Kumbla: Caribbean Women and Literature,* edited by Carole Boyce Davies and Elaine Savory Fido, Africa World Press, 355–72.